AF064546

Concern for Creation

Tim Matton-Johnson

Concern for Creation

Living on country in a 21st century way

Tim Matton-Johnson

Adelaide
2025

©copyright remains with Tim Matton-Johnson

All rights reserved. No part of this publication may be reproduced, stored in a retrieval system, or transmitted, in any form or by any means, electronic, mechanical, photocopying, recording or otherwise, without the prior written permission of the publishers.

ISBN:
978-1-923385-14-6   Softcover
978-1-923385-15-3   Hardcover
978-1-923385-16-0   Epub
978-1-923385-17-7   PDF

Published by:

Making a lasting impact
An imprint of the ATF Press Publishing Group
owned by ATF (Australia) Ltd.
PO Box 234
Brompton, SA 5007
Australia
ABN 90 116 359 963
www.atfpress.com

Table of Contents

Introduction		ix
	Living on country in a twenty-first century way	ix
	Personal history of reclamation of Aboriginal identity	xi
	Outlining the scope of this book	xvi

Part 1 Climate Change and Associated Issues

Chapter 1	**Existential Crisis**	**1**
	Complexity of the Issues	1
	The Ecological Crisis	1
	Advancing Technology and Climate Change	6
	National Sovereignty and Climate Change	8
	Popular Aspirations and Climate Change	9
Chapter 2	**Economics, Resilience and Climate Change**	**13**
	Political Economy	13
	Rising inequality	16
	Resilience	20
Chapter 3	**Indigenous Knowledges**	**25**
	A More Sustainable Way	25
	Conclusions for Part One	33

Part 2 Invasion and Response—Woorrady

Chapter 4	**Exploring the theology of Woorrady**	**37**
	Epistemological Issues	37
	Devils, Spirit or being?	40
Chapter 5	**Woorrady's Theology**	**47**
	1838 Sermons	47
	Who was this man?	48

	The broader historical and theological perspective	49
	What does the text, the synopsis of Woorrady's sermon tell us?	54
Chapter 6	**Conversations on the theme of Creation July 1831**	**59**
	Introduction to the Texts	59
	Reflecting on this series of conversations	63
Chapter 7	**Return to 1838 and the Sermon**	**73**
	Accommodation or Critique?	73
	Conclusions and possible ways forward	78

Part 3 The God-Creation Story (Christian Perspective)

Chapter 8	**Introduction**	**83**
	Bringing the Story up to Date	84
	Almost up to Date	90
Chapter 9	**Wraerggowrapper—Philosophical and Scientific responses**	**99**
	The problem of Evil	99
	Quantum Uncertainty	103
	Self-organisation	109
	Genetics—Do our Genes determine our future?	114
Chapter 10	**Wraeggowraper—Biblical and Theological responses**	**119**
	Some Epistemological Matters	119
	Book of Job	120
	Moltmann's Trinitarian theology of the Cross	124
	Where have we Travelled so Far in this Section?	131
Chapter 11	**Resurrection and New Creation**	**133**
	Beginning with Paul	133
	Resurrection Accounts in the Gospels	140
	The Gospel Accounts through the eyes of Paul	145
Chapter 12	**Trinitarian Eschatology**	**151**
	Moltmann's Critique of Political and Theological Monotheism	151
	Moltmann's Trinitarian Eschatology	154
	Creation as God's Project	157

Part 4 Reflections on the Journey

Chapter 13	**Bringing the Threads Together**	**165**
	Reflecting on Christian Theology in an aboriginal way	165
	Reflections on the Ecological challenges to our current way of life	169
	Voice	176
Bibliography		**181**

Introduction

Living on country in a twenty-first century way

I have always believed that in some way everything is connected to everything else. I also recognise that the limitations of one person's life means that a comprehensive theory of everything is an impossible task. This piece of writing is simply an attempt to connect together some themes that have become significant in shaping my spirituality as an Aboriginal Christian living in a world that is entering into a time of great challenge.

For the last few years, I have been experimenting with something called 'living on country in a twenty-first century way'. Where I got that name from, I am not sure. I don't think I invented it! So much has changed over the two centuries or so from the way of living with country/land of precolonial times. So how, in these very different circumstances we find ourselves in today, do we develop a relationship with country/land: how might we develop a relationship that informs us at multiple levels, socially, spiritually, intellectually, and physically? How do you do that in a very different context? One thing for sure is that I could end up annoying my neighbours considerably if I started using fire as a land management tool! There are also many other structures and underlying assumptions within contemporary society and mainstream civilization that make it difficult to think about living on country/land in a pre-colonial way. But are there not some principles from the old ways that still work? How then does one learn to love the country/land you are on? Special places, sacred sites, the mountains, the tall forests, pristine beaches, places that inspire and lift the heart are easy to love. But how do you love the places where you live and work? Sometimes where we spend most of our lives feels much smaller and removed from nature. We might be living in a high-rise apartment somewhere in the middle of a big city, or sometimes, like me, on a rural residential property where you have a few more options but are still constrained by the regulations and conventions of mainstream society.

On our half a hectare block I have been experimenting with trying to enhance the life of the country/land I am on. I try to think about it in two ways. Thinking about it in terms of the block of land that the house is on and at the same time thinking about it as the whole of ecosphere earth. So, I try to do things that are ecologically good things to be doing both locally and as a small contribution to the global effort. In terms of technology, we included such things as solar panels, good insulation, double glazing and orienting the house to the sun to try and maximise energy efficiency. I could not help noticing that most of the other owners, on what was still a new estate, did not bother with much with these kinds of measures. Given more than half a hectare to play with, yet they still oriented their houses to the boundary whichever direction that happened to be pointing. It was as though they were still in suburbia on blocks a tenth of the size, having little thought for things like passive solar gain in the winter.

When it comes to working ecologically, we started with a patch of grazing land. The plan was to grow some of our own food and to find ways to enhance the ecosystem by planting trees and shrubs, including a high proportion of native species. We also wanted to try some endangered Tasmanian native species. One of these was the Morrisby Gum. We are a little outside its natural range, but they seemed to work ok. I became emotionally impacted in a good way over time with these trees. A couple of years ago two of these Morrisby Gums flowered and last summer I was able to collect some seed from them. I was able to propagate the seed. Now I've got second generation trees on our property.

From the practical point of view, I am not engineer, a gardener or a horticulturalist. I am not professionally trained in any appropriate discipline for implementing or designing many of the ideas that have been a part of developing the block. The point is if an amateur like me can make progress on living on country/land in a twenty-first century way all of us can. We will return to this practical theme later. For now, it is important to give some insight into the perspective from which this book is written by way of understanding the cultural dimension which shapes my thinking as a person of aboriginal heritage living in the land of my ancestors.

While this book is basically concerned with theology the reader will notice that other disciplines, such as history, economics, and science, appear from time to time. There will also be passages of my own spirituality and life journey appearing here and there. The theme that everything is connected is at the base of aboriginal thought. A range of voices need to be heard to provide context and connection for a theology that might shape life. The reader is invited into this way of thinking through the theology not as a siloed discipline but as something that is intimately connected to the reality of life lived in our times. With this in mind it is important introduce myself a little before continuing this introduction.

Personal history of reclamation of Aboriginal identity

When I first began engaging with UAICC Tasmania a couple of the elders challenged me to do family research to find out what connection, if any, I had to early colonial history. Two connections were uncovered. First, the story of my ancestor Mary Ann Coates, a Tasmanian Aboriginal girl stolen from her people. The other was the story of the McCoy family. They arrived in Tasmania as free settlers from Ireland and were granted fifty acres of land, not very far from where I now live. It is possible but difficult to prove that they could have been involved in 'clearing' the 'natives' out of the district. It is possible that they could have also been part of the black line. This was the biggest mobilisation per capita ever in Australia, with the objective of removing all the remaining Aboriginal people from the 'settled districts' of Van Diemen's Land. It was not a very successful strategy, but it was a very determined effort.

Learning about Mary Ann was not entirely a surprise. There were pointers and hints in this direction here and there since early childhood.

Perhaps the earliest of these was a story that my mother used to tell whenever the subject of family history came up. She would tell us the story that her grandmother used to say to her that she must have been swapped in the hospital. This related to the fact that she was born with dark hair, olive skin and brown eyes. Whereas her sister was blonde, fair skinned and blue eyed, like the rest of the family. When mum told this story she was clearly troubled by it and interpreting it to mean that she didn't belong. It was only years later that I began to understand that there was something racist underlying this story. Great grandmother was clearly concerned that mum's appearance might well bring back into the light of day some sort of mixed race but deeply buried incident in the family history. Mum was born in 1934 just one year after Adolf Hitler had become chancellor of Germany. At a time when most major Western powers had racist policies of some sort. Any notion of an Aboriginal connexion anywhere in the family could have significant downside for the children. Great grandma wanted this story to stay buried, for very good reasons.

Another pointer in this direction was the family's willingness to have Aboriginal children from the Methodist missions coming to stay with us during school holidays. I can remember at least five different children coming to stay with us between about 1960 to the early 70s. It was only much later that I realised these children were a part of what we now know as the stolen generation. Why else would they have come to us for holidays and not returned to their own communities and families?

When I was in primary school in grade four, we were taught quite clearly that there were no Aboriginal people in Tasmania. This had been so since the death of Truganina almost 100 years before. That same year I had the opportunity to visit Flinders Island on the Anzac Day long weekend. My stepfather was an Air Force chaplain so was leading the service. As a part of the service all the school children lined up on the parade ground. I could not help but notice many Aboriginal faces amongst the children. I questioned this. My stepfather responded by saying, 'they're not really Aboriginal children they are octoroons'. This is a very difficult and racist word. Thankfully it is not heard very often these days. To call people this is a dehumanising phrase. From that time, I began to question the history I was being taught in school.

Another feature of my childhood was the beginning of spirituality focused on creation and country/land. As a four-year-old, I was out with my father and older brother on the farm. It was lambing season. We came across a sheep giving birth. My father called us both over to witness the birth. I was distracted by seeing sunlight coming through the clouds in that particular manner that was used in the style of artwork from my children's Bible to indicate an epiphany. When I got there the lamb had just been born. My brother said that I had missed it. I spoke up and said I had seen it coming from God. My father was a Methodist lay preacher and simply accepted my statement as valid. In a four-year-old way I was already engaging in creation theology.

Just a few months later my father, Jack Matton, died suddenly in the middle of the night. This event had a profound impact on all of our lives. Back in 1961 it was not the 'done thing' for young children to attend funerals. Mum had felt uneasy about this. in response she decided to take us to visit the grave after she had picked us up from the babysitters. She claimed that the short sermon I gave in the car on the way home from the visit to the cemetery was much better than the one she heard in the funeral service. The toddler theologian in action again! I can still picture the occasion but have no memory of what I actually said.

The next thing that happened was our foster sister was removed from the family after being with us for two years or so. Mum had become a young widow with four small children to look after. The youngest, my sister, was only five months old and had a serious heart condition. She also found herself with a dairy farm to manage. And much later I discovered that she was also having to deal with predatory males who saw a young widow as a legitimate target. She managed for a little over two years but in the end decided to sell up and move to the city. Shortly after this she remarried a very different kind of man than her first husband.

During this time my spirituality of creation/country/land began to develop in an unusual way. After reflection I think that what happened was the basic trust that had been centred on my father became increasingly centred on Tasmania's Mountain country/land. Two trips to cradle mountain as a six-year-old were significant in this process. Of special note, on the first trip, is when, for the first time, I walked through a patch of rainforest as the sun came through the leaves. It was like walking into a cathedral, a holy place. All the different shades of green and brown, of Moss and lichen bark and leaves. It seemed to me to be a place of safety and wonder.

It is about this time that my habit of looking into country/land, examining my feelings and asking questions of country/land began. Simple questions like; am I safe here? do I feel at home? do I feel welcome? or do I feel somehow an alien? Asking questions and seeking answers; all part of establishing a relationship with country/land wherever I was.

While I was not surprised to discover Aboriginal connection all the way back to Mary Ann, the question of identification as an Aboriginal person was not so simple. There were two reasons for this. Firstly, there was no connexion I could find between Mary Ann and the better-known Aboriginal groups whose descent clearly went back to colonial times. Second, there was a large gap between my generation and my grandmother's generation during which the Aboriginal connexion was a closely guarded secret. By the time my research had identified Mary Ann as Aboriginal, I could no longer ask my grandmother for further information. She had died some years earlier. Had she known something about the decision to hide this connection, she had kept it quiet. Within the context of identity politics, both within and outside of the Tasmanian Aboriginal community, this gap of at least two generations, I felt, at the time, this would make it difficult to argue a strong case re cultural continuity. Consequently it seemed best not to self-identify.

Over the next couple of years, I was twice identified as Aboriginal by community elders despite having not told them anything about my family history. The first time was during a session break at a meeting in Melbourne. An Aboriginal elder from Robinvale up on the Murray River told me that by looking into my eyes she could tell I was Aboriginal. I was totally unsure how to handle this and struggled to understand how such a thing could even be possible. So, I again stayed silent about my family history.

The second occasion was far more significant. In mid-2007 Lynne and I were in Darwin at UCA Ministers' conference which was centred around the theme of covenanting between the UCA and the Aboriginal and Islander Christian Congress. We had also elected to go on an extension tour following the conference. This tour took us to Yirrkala, in Yolngu country/land (East Arnhem Land). We were there for several days as a part of the community. During this stay I could sense that our group of ministers, of which we were a part, was being closely observed and, at times, even tested by various elders.

While we were there, the newly elected Prime Minister, Keven Rudd, decided to hold his first 'Community Cabinet meeting' in Yirrkala. This caused a change of plans for our tour. Originally, we were meant to meet with some elders on an outstation, but this became impossible because all the elders were coming into Yirrkala to present ideas to the cabinet. Instead of flying to an outstation, we were invited to sit in and listen to them as they met to decide what they would bring up with the Prime Minister and cabinet. However, this also had to change because some government officials also wanted to be in on this meeting.

The elders clearly did not want these officials briefing the Prime Minster on their discussions. But if we were invited to listen then how could they be refused? It was decided that all should leave after the formal opening of the meeting. I wondered how this could be done in a proper respectful way. When I was picked by the Chairman of the meeting to open the meeting with prayer it dawned on me that I was the one picked to manage this exit in the proper way. I led what I thought was an appropriate prayer, then shook hands with the elder closest to me and then continued shaking hands all around the circle and realised that all the others, both ministers and the officials were following me around and out the door. If this was a test, I think I passed!

On the last night we were there we had a farewell gathering with all the people we had met. Lynne and I were sitting opposite a couple of elders we had spent much of our time with during the visit. Towards the end of our meal the husband leaned across the table and touched me on the arm and said, 'My wife thinks you are Aboriginal'. I had been avoiding telling anyone about my family history but felt after this statement I had to open up. I told them the story of Mary Ann and they were both delighted by this confirmation of their insight.

It was only much later that I realised that it may not have been the conversations and my passing the obvious test, that in the end, led to this identification as Aboriginal. One of the other things I was frequently doing on this trip was looking into country/land in the way I described earlier as a lifetime habit. I would have been observed doing this and maybe it was a clue that revealed the nature of my relation to country/land as having Aboriginal character.

Not long after this Yirrkala visit the issue of self-identification came up in the context of UAICC TAS committee meeting. We were discussing who might go to the next national conference. Only Aboriginal delegates could vote at these conferences. If I was prepared to self-identify and this was endorsed by our elder, then I could be accepted as Aboriginal for the purposes of this conference. One of the other Aboriginal men in the meeting warned me that identifying could lead to a world of pain, from racism and the politics of identity.

He was dead right about this. But after being identified as Aboriginal twice by elders from two completely different parts of Australia how could I not start down this journey into ancient identity that was to be overfilled with both moments of, belonging and joy, and also deep pain? I do not regret choosing to identify even though it has been a roller-coaster ride.

Outlining the scope of this book

I have come to understand myself as both an Aboriginal person and a Christian theologian. I have learnt much about the Aboriginal culture and long history of our people in this land. I have also been educated by the western university system with its emphasis on critical thinking. There is a strong sense in which my life has been a walking in two cultures. In the chapters that follow the perspective of what is written will therefore reflect both. It is the intention to explore the theology and spirituality that underpins what I call living on country/land in a twenty-first century way. I believe that this project is of vital importance as the world faces the challenge of climate change and ecological collapse.

In the first part of this book, I will try to describe, what has been described as the existential threat of our time, climate change and the implications it may have for human civilisation. At the moment, it seems that this crisis is largely being seen in terms of a technological issue on which considerable progress is and can be made. However, without major cultural, economic, and political changes to address the major drivers that have brought us all into this space, advances in technology will not save us from disaster.

There is also need for significant cultural change in the way we go about human civilisation. It is not incremental change or tinkering around the edges of our current civilisation but change that is transformative and leads towards a whole different way of being a human community living on the a planet that is an ecological marvel.

It is not the intention of this book to provide a comprehensive account of the current state of play on all of the complexity of issues involved in the ecological crisis we face. I do not have the level of expertise needed to do so. Instead, the intention is to provide enough commentary such that a realistic understanding of the situation can be achieved, without too much blame and fear. I will also try to point towards positive work already begun by others in order to allow some room for hope rather than fuelling despair and tempting readers to put it all into the 'to hard basket'.

In the second part of this book, I will explore my aboriginal self-understanding by working with the theology of Woorrady. He was a Nuenonne man from Southeast Tasmania. He lived from circa 1790 to 1842 and was a witness to the almost total destruction of the Tasmanian Aboriginal people, their culture and country/land. I will use his traditional stories, as recorded in colonial records, as a theological case study.

In the third part of the book, I will explore a particular theme that emerges from this traditional Aboriginal theology, the Wraeggowraper designation. In western philosophy the closest parallel to this is usually know as 'the problem of evil' or 'why do good people suffer from evil'. This theme will be worked through from the perspective of western philosophy, scientific ways of understanding our world, biblical and theological responses to this theme. The intention is to eventually illuminate a way of living meaningfully with hope through the challenges of the future.

It is hoped that this will bring a renewed focus on a way of understanding our world through a spirituality that begins to change personal attitudes towards country/land may assist larger social change in ways that provide for a more hopeful transition over the coming decades of increasing challenge. Changing hearts and minds needs to be a part of the process. The practice of learning to live on country/land in a twenty-first century way has certainly begun to change me in holistic ways. There has been a distinct shift in my emotional, spiritual, and physical lifestyle.

Part 1 Climate Change and Associated Issues

Chapter 1
Existential Crisis

Complexity of the Issues

Planet Earth and its human civilisation is facing its biggest crisis in ten thousand years on multiple fronts. Global warming is changing the climate at a rate that is putting the whole planet's ecosystem under increasing stress. Loss of ecological diversity is lowering the resilience of critical ecosystems. Increasing inequity both within national economies and between them is putting increased stress on vulnerable populations. The list goes on and it is the scale and type of activity of our current human global systems that is the root cause of this developing challenge.

In this section we want to examine the ecological crisis that the world is currently facing. This will focus on a description of the ecological crisis that we face, possible technological solutions, and efforts to reform, even transform, the nature of the civilisation which has brought about this ecological crisis.

The Ecological Crisis

So, what is this ecological crisis? In her book, *Doughnut Economics*, Kate Raworth[1] lists nine externalities that go beyond what she calls the safe ecological ceiling, which is the space outside of the safe doughnut. It is worth listing them. They are ozone layer depletion, air pollution, biodiversity loss, land conversion, freshwater withdrawals, nitrogen and phosphorus loading, chemical pollution, ocean acidification, and the big one, climate change. When we turn to the Appendix of Kate's

---
1. Kate Raworth, *Doughnut Economics* (London: Penguin, 2017).

book, we can find brief explanations of these nine items. Raworth attributes these nine externalities to an international group of Earth-system scientists led by Johan Rockstrom and Will Steffen.

> *Ozone layer depletion.* Earth's stratospheric ozone layer filters out ultraviolet radiation from the sun. some human-made chemical substances such as chlorofluorocarbons (CFC's) will, if released, into the stratosphere and deplete the ozone layer, exposing earth and its inhabitants to the sun's harmful UV rays.
>
> *Air pollution.* Micro-particles, or aerosols, emitted into the air—such as smoke, dust and pollutant gases—can damage living organisms. Furthermore, they interact with water vapour in the air and affect cloud formation. When emitted in large volumes these aerosols can significantly alter regional rainfall patterns, including shifting the timing and location of monsoon rains in tropical regions.
>
> *Biodiversity loss.* A decline in the number and variety of living species damages the integrity of ecosystems and accelerates species extinction. In doing so it increases the risk of abrupt and irreversible changes to ecosystems, reducing their resilience and undermining their capacity to provide food, fuel and fibre, and to sustain life.
>
> *Land conversion* Converting land for human use—such as turning forests and wetlands into cities farmland and highways—depletes Earth's carbon sinks, destroys rich wildlife habitats and undermines the land's role in continually cycling water nitrogen and phosphorus.
>
> *Freshwater withdrawals.* Water is essential for life and is widely used by agriculture, industry and households. Excessive withdrawals of water, however, can impair or even dry up lakes, rivers and aquifers, damaging ecosystems and altering the hydrological cycle and climate.
>
> *Nitrogen and phosphorus loading.* reactive nitrogen and phosphorus are widely used in agricultural fertilisers but only a small proportion of what is applied is actually taken up by crops. Most of the access runs off into rivers, lakes and oceans, where it causes algae blooms that turn the water green. These

blooms can be toxic and they kill off other aquatic life by starving it of oxygen.

Chemical pollution. when toxic compounds, such as synthetic organic pollutants and heavy metals, are released into the biosphere they can persist for a very long time, with effects that may be irreversible. And when they accumulate in the tissue of living creatures, including birds and mammals, they reduce fertility and cause genetic damage, endangering ecosystems on land and in the oceans.

Ocean acidification. Around one quarter of the carbon dioxide admitted by human activity is eventually dissolved in the oceans, where it forms carbonic acid and decreases the pH of the surface water. This acidity reduces the availability of carbonate ions that are an essential building block used by many marine species for shell and skeleton formation. This missing ingredient makes it hard for organisms such as corals, shellfish and plankton to grow and survive, thus endangering the ocean ecosystem and its food chain.

Climate change. When the greenhouse gases such as carbon dioxide, methane and nitrous oxide are released into the air, they enter the atmosphere and amplify Earth's natural greenhouse effect trapping more heat within the atmosphere. This results in global warming, whose effects include rising temperatures, more frequent extremes of weather, and sea level rise.[2]

Of these nine environmental challenges only one is diminishing. All the rest are still growing. The Ozone layer depletion is the only one where there are indications are of slow improvement. This is because once it was understood that the use of CFCs was the primary cause of its depletion, banning their use and finding alternatives to their use in refrigeration systems and aerosol products was a relatively simple fix and soon implemented. Two of these nine externalities do not have defined planetary boundaries against which progress can be measured. They are chemical pollution (which would include plastics pollution) and air pollution. This means that we simply don't know how much there is, or what a safe level might be.

---

2. Raworth, *Doughnut Economics*, 297–298.

In the centre of her Doughnut Kate Raworth places a number of shortfalls that reflect the United Nations sustainable development goals. These include access to basic human needs. The list includes education, income and work, peace and justice, political voice, social equity, gender equity, housing, networks, energy, water, food and health.[3] This is a list of things that ought to be available to all human beings in a more just society. However, there are billions of people whose lives are threatened, or diminished, by the lack of one or more of these shortfalls. There is a lack of equity or fairness in this story that to some extent exists in every society. This unfairness can be seen as another externality that poses a serious threat to mainstream human civilisation and ecological sustainability on Earth.

While recognising the multifaceted ecological challenges that we face, let us now turn to the challenge of climate change in particular. At the most recent international conference on climate change all countries were asked to participate and make commitments on reaching net zero carbon emissions by 2050. This target arises out of the Kyoto and Paris protocols. It allows for a global rise in average temperature of 1.5 degrees Celsius above the 1980s average by 2050. This might not sound all that much but it is not a return to the Holocene average over the past 10,000 years or so that has been so advantageous for human civilisation. We would need an eighteenth century pre-industrial base line get back to that point. However, it was considered that this target was achievable and would significantly prevent climate change spiralling out of control.

Most nations were represented at this conference but not all committed to the proposed target. Some nations, amongst those still working on developing their economies, wanted more time. In particular the world two most populated countries, China and India. China committed to 2060 and India saw 2070 as more likely. In recent decades both of these countries have developed their economies by encouraging much more private enterprise as the dynamism for economic growth. Hundreds of millions of their citizens have significantly improved their economic status to something more like the middleclass lifestyles more typical of the more developed economies of the west. However, they both still have far more people living in poverty. It is easy to understand how both of these nations,

---

3. Raworth, *Doughnut Economics*, 44.

and other smaller nations experiencing the same 'only part way there' development status also would like more time. This is especially so when it was not them but todays "developed nations" who started these unsustainable development trends.

A recent forecast by the United Nations meteorological department, noting the recent shift from the La Nina to the El Nino pattern in the Pacific Ocean, suggested that in the next five-year period we may see the first 1.5 C target reached for the first time. This may not stabilise there yet. There could be a ten-or twenty-year period of fluctuation around that level before it becomes the average. Two degrees Celsius in 2070 is beginning to look more likely as the time and level that may constitute net zero.

In March 2023 the United Nations' International Panel on Climate Change issued its sixth report (AR6). This report gave some potentially scary statistics and predictions. The two that struck me in this way were the numbers of people who were already at risk of adverse effects of climate change and the long-term effects, particularly the build-up of sea level rise. These adverse risks include, sea-level rises, coastal flooding caused by high tides being pushed further inland by storm surges of increasingly more powerful storms, more intense flooding, more frequent droughts, heatwaves, more severe wildfires (especially those in forest ecologies where fires were not part of normal cycles). The report puts the number of people currently at risk of these sorts of events, which we are already seeing many every year in some part of the world, at 3.6 billion. That is roughly more than forty per cent of the world's current population living in current at-risk situations.

The report also estimates the period of slowly rising sea levels before stabilisation after some 2000 years. Apparently, this is because it takes a very long time for warmer ocean surface temperatures to reach all the way down into the deep oceans. Water incrementally expands as it warms. The loss of the Greenland icecap, and part or all the Antarctic icecap anytime during that long period will exacerbate the situation.

If these above issues are not scary enough there is also another timing issue that is relevant to all of this. Net zero is not the end of the story. It is but the first major step on a much longer journey. Eventually we will need to draw down the greenhouse gases in the atmosphere not just stop them from rising. This will probably take centuries rather than decades. One of the best known and easiest ways of sequestering carbon from the atmosphere is reafforestation. However, it takes time to plant and regrow forests. Some trees take hundreds of years to grow to full size. Composting, making biochar by slow burning, ploughing in stubble are all quicker and smaller scale ways of trapping carbon into soil. Again, it may take centuries to make an appreciable difference. Despite the long timeframe all these methods should be taken up. There is also some science being done around the possibility of direct carbon capture from the atmosphere and storage below ground. However, it is still at an early stage, and it is not yet clear how practical this might be.

Advancing Technology and Climate Change

Technological approaches to climate change, and other environmental challenges, are happening on many levels. In the search for energy sources that do not rely on fossil fuels work has been going on for some time. We have seen in recent years energy production from wind and solar increasing to the point where both are beginning to make significant contributions towards society's energy usage. Large scale battery systems have also begun to store and distribute energy from these sources in a more efficient manner. There are also other green energy projects that as yet are not in this post development and scale up situation. Pumped Hydro is also being looked at was a way of building on existing infrastructure. This is basically about using excess solar or wind energy to pump water from hydroelectric production back up into the storage dams, to integrate these three forms of energy production. In Queensland there is an energy company, Genex Power, which is developing an old mine site into a green energy hub. As well as the pumped hydro project they are also using a large-scale battery system, wind and solar farms on a scale that could power a medium sized city. However not all Hydro plants are suitable for this type of development. This circular use of water could significantly reduce down stream flows and exacerbate both environmental flows and human water usage. Careful individual assessment is needed for pumped hydro schemes.

There are also a number of projects looking at green energy that as yet have not developed as far as solar, wind and hydro. Some have been looking at tide and wave power plants but so far have not been able to bring them to a level of reliability for scaling up in significant ways.

There was also a recent announcement by scientists investigating fusion power. They had finally managed to get more power out of their prototype reactor than they had to put in, but only a fraction. Getting a stable reaction over long lengths of time that produces significantly more energy than it uses is still perhaps decades off. Another one that may be more promising, in terms of time scales, is the production of green hydrogen as an alternative to fossil fuels. Hydrogen is normally produced by electrolysis where electricity is used to split water atoms with oxygen as by product. This may be problematic if we have to use green electricity to get our fuel. There is a South Australian Company, Sparc Energy, which is developing a 'green hydrogen' process which uses photocatalytic water splitting via a solar reactor to produce hydrogen and oxygen from water directly from sun light without the need for electricity. This technology is still at the stage of testing a commercial scale reactor, but could be promising.

The burning of hydrogen releases a considerable amount of energy. Approximately four times as much carbon-based fuels. The resultant by product is more water. There is a need for redesign. It is not possible to simply use hydrogen in engines designed for oil or gas because of this dramatically higher energy yield. The development of hydrogen fuel cells to produce electricity for electric vehicles as a recharge for the batteries as you drive is seen as a possible way to extend the range of such vehicles.

Another issue that comes up in this context is recycling. It seems that our current system is very good at coming up with all sorts of new products but not anywhere near as good at recycling old or worn-out stuff. Part of the problem is in the economics of the process. Many of the products that can end up needing recycling have many components that need to be sorted back into raw materials. Often this is not easy to do and, if it can be done, the cost of producing these renewed raw materials is far greater than that of getting them out of the ground in the first place. Ought there be some sort of levy introduced earlier in the life cycle of raw materials in order to support their eventual recycling?

Having looked at the issue of climate change from the perspective of emerging technologies what can we say? There is some hope that we may develop a basket of technological ideas and processes that will help mitigate the effects of climate change. However, all of these technologies take time to develop and scale up to the point where they can get us to net zero and beyond. This transition may take several decades. Again, this is an indication that things may well get worse before we reach net zero.

National Sovereignty and Climate Change

When we come to looking at the ways in which our mainstream human civilisation functions, we find within it forces that are both causes and continuing powerful drivers of the crisis we face. We see this in increasing social and economic inequity. This inequity can be observed in almost every nation on earth. It also continues to exist the international context between rich and poor nations. We see further symptoms in our politics. In the two hundred or so sovereign nation states in the world there is not a consensus on just how such states should govern themselves. All reserve the right to make their own rules. There are some hereditary monarchies, only some of these are constitutional in nature. Many of these independent states are republican in style but again there is a great deal of variation. Some have powerful presidents who can behave in autocratic ways, obtaining multiple terms with the support of power bases like the very wealthy and or military establishments. Others are more traditional democracies with constitutional separations of powers between the judiciary, elected parliamentary representation and executive government. Even many of these are struggling with both the current Geopolitical environment and the multiple environmental issues involving global challenges.

While there are many variations in the styles of national governments around the world, they all share a similar understanding of the idea of national sovereignty. This means they reserve the right to govern their territory and those who live there under their own laws and to protect what they determine as their national interests, and even what they may term national aspirations. There does exist a body of international law that is called upon to resolve disputes between nations. However, these can be hard to enforce, especially when some nations refuse to sign up international covenants. And there are even cases where nations might sign up but fail to enforce in their own jurisdictions. Unfortunately, Climate change and the other associated externalities know nothing of international borders.

This sovereignty issue is partly the reason behind the widely different net zero targets that came out of the climate summit mentioned earlier. It is also behind some earlier attempts to 'export' the problem. For quite some time Australia tried to do this. Recycling was exported to some of the poorer Southeast Asian countries. Where some of the higher value items (particularly metals) could indeed be extracted from the piles of plastic. Labour was cheap and health and safety of workers often not thought about. However, there was a lot of rubbish, particularly plastics, that could not be recycled in low tech ways that just piled up and polluted the local environment. Eventually these poor countries banned such imports. Another example of this 'export the problem' was the failed attempt of the Rudd—Gillard labour government's attempt to put a price on carbon, or tax the extraction of fossil fuels more than a decade ago. Our production of fossil fuels was not seen to be part of the problem, only the actual users of them was seen to be relevant. Essentially the end user was handed the entire cost of cleaning up while we pocketed the profits. Between them the big producers of coal and gas and our conservative politicians campaigned against it successfully. Subsequently a conservative government was elected, and a decade of inaction followed. With three consecutive conservative governments there was a lack of any substantive action on climate change.

We will come back to the problematic nature of national sovereignty in a later chapter. It is enough now to tag it as another issue in approaching the many global environmental challenges that we face.

Popular Aspirations and Climate Change

One further issue that needs to be mentioned is one from the other end of the spectrum from the international. This is the role of individual aspirations in helping to fuel the externalities we face. Most of us aspire for a better life, or a better life for our children. We want to be successful in life. This, in itself, is not a bad thing but the way it is seen, measured, or symbolised can be an issue. Increasingly for people all over the world success is being measured in terms of individual materialism. Everything from having the latest cool gadget to bigger and more fashionable housing. This has been going on for many generations and continues to accelerate. There is also a very persuasive advertising and promotional industry making sure that we all know about the latest trends and appliances.

Housing in Australia provides an interesting case study of this materialist acceleration. In the post WW II decades, when broad scale suburban housing took off, the typical 'quarter acre block' (roughly 800 square metres) was used for each house. The typical three bedroomed house had a total floor area of about 100 square metres. Families moving into these homes typically included two adults and anywhere between two and six children of varying ages. Most families only had one car. Today the situation is significantly different. Average block sizes have halved to about 400 square metres while house sizes have virtually doubled. This reduces available green space in the new suburbs by a huge margin. The average number of people living in such houses is now less than 2.5 and at the same time the number of vehicles per household has more than doubled. The orientation of the blocks and the houses on them is controlled not by passive solar gain, suitability for solar panels or summer cooling, but by the most efficient layout of streets. The double garage is a must have and the only place to put is on the ground floor at the front of the house. It sometimes seems that planning is more about cars than people. The lack of green space in such suburbs increases flash flooding during heavy rainfall events and raises the temperature during heat waves. In short, more resources to house less people. As global warming continues the people who live in these newer suburbs are put at greater risk and have less options to counter these risks. Larger sized housing of course is also about the aspirations of people to have something more than the previous generation. But in a sense, they are getting yesterday's housing instead of resilient housing for the future.

To add to these issues around the way we are currently doing housing, is a current housing crisis brought on by the effects of covid 19. A great deal of government money was poured into the economy in attempts to keep it going during the lockdowns. A large amount of this often badly targeted stimulus found its way into assets like housing. At the same time much construction was slowed so the existing stock became more valuable overnight. The market tightened rapidly, and construction only ramped up slowly because of extended supply chain issues as the world economy re-emerged from the pandemic at different rates across many countries. Add to all this a quick return of immigration there was a sudden rise in demand, far out stripping supply. One aspect of this was a decline in affordability for many families.

The high number of houses with spare rooms, because there are only couples or singles living in them, since their children have moved away, may seem a possible solution. However, because the way we have done it since WW II nearly all the housing in suburbs is of similar kind. Downsizing by older couples frequently means that they will need to move to new communities rather than stay in the same community, close to the decades old relationships that are a significant part of their ongoing lives. In some communities there are simply no units or townhouses to downsize into.

What do we take from all of this with respect to climate change. What seems at first sight to be reasonable aspirations of ordinary people, if they are based around any sort of material success, no matter small, will have an impact on human society's resilience in the face of climate change and all its ecological externalities. We can also note the importance of relationships built up over many years as a part the reluctance of older people may have to moving away from their larger family homes. This is an aspect of what can be thought of as relational wealth, a completely different worthwhile measure of a successful life. We will come back to this thought later on.

Chapter 2
Economics, Resilience and Climate Change

Political Economy

The one area in which there seems to be considerable like-mindedness between nations is economic policy. Most of the nations of the world seem to favour economic growth as the most important national goal. So, let us begin with a closer look at economics.

Kate Raworth's book, 'Doughnut Economics' has a subtitle, 'Seven Ways to Think Like a 21st Century Economist'.[1] Each chapter looks at one of these seven ways. The first chapter heading is 'Change the Goal from GDP to the Doughnut'. GDP is gross domestic product. It is simply a way to measure the size of a national economy. It is not a measure of the quality of an economy, just current size. It will tell us nothing about how the actual citizens of any country are faring in the economy, who is getting rich and who is struggling with poverty or anything else about the quality of life, and certainly not anything about the ecological health of the country.

In 2014 the leaders of the world's twenty largest national economies (by the GDP measure) met in Brisbane to discuss a range of economic and trade issues. In their joint public statement, they resolved to work together towards at target of 2.1% increase in world GDP. In her introduction to this chapter Kate makes these comments in regard to this 2014 G20 goal.

> How did it come to this? The G20's pledge was announced just days after the Intergovernmental Panel on Climate Change warned that the world faces 'severe, pervasive and

---
1. Raworth, *Doughnut Economics*.

irreversible' damage from rising greenhouse gas emissions. But the summit's Australian host, then Prime Minister Tony Abbott, had been determined to stop the meeting's agenda from being 'cluttered' by climate change and other issues that could distract from his top priority of economic growth, otherwise known as GDP growth.[2]

So where did this idea of economic growth as the core priority of national governments come from? Kate points out that it first emerged in the USA during the 1930 great depression as a way of tracking the success, or lack of success, of government policy as it tried to find its way out of that depression.[3] GDP growth was never intended to be the goal of economic policy. Reducing chronic unemployment and the resulting widespread poverty of the depression and the general welfare of the population was the goal. Change in GDP, year by year, was just a way of measuring the success of overall economic policy. It was not intended to be the actual purpose of economic activity.

Kate Raworth further comments,

> And so after half a century, GDP growth shifted from being a policy option to a political necessity, and the de facto policy goal. To inquire weather further growth was always desirable, necessary, or indeed possible, became irrelevant, or political suicide.[4]

One of the main issues with making growth the central purpose and goal of the global economic system is the ignoring of limits. The earth, and its ecology, is a finite system so there must be a limit, even if not well defined, to the size and growth of human civilisation. The recent increases in extreme climate events may well the first signs that we are getting very close to such limits, if not crossing some not easy to return from boundaries. It is also worth noting that GDP is not the only economic measure that we should be concerned about. GDP is an income measure and as such, from an accounting perspective, belongs on the profit and loss statement. We also need to be concerned about the health of our balance sheet where assets and liabilities are measured, and net wealth can be determined.

---

2. Raworth, *Doughnut Economics*, 31.
3. Raworth, *Doughnut Economics*, 36.
4. Raworth, *Doughnut Economics*, 40.

There are two types of enterprises that need to provide a full set of financial accounts each year. They are businesses who seek to generate surpluses (usually called profits) and not for profit organisations who also seek to achieve surpluses. However, they use their surpluses in quite different ways. Businesses will generally use part of their profits to pay dividends to their shareholders, the rest may be used to pay down debts and or reinvest in their business operations. Not for profits will generally use all surpluses to reinvest into the purposes for which they were originally set up. While NGOs may have members with an annual subscription, they do not have shareholders who expect a return on their investment.

The profit and loss statement will show all the various types of income received during the year and all the expenses involved with their operations. There may also be some accruals which are incomes and expenses entered into by way of contracts to buy or sell for a known price that has not yet been paid. On the balance sheet we may also see some assets and liabilities that do not have a value determined by specific financial transaction. These are given fair estimations on the basis of agreed accounting standards. Intellectual property such as product patents and copywrite licences are an example of these types of assets. Provisions for future costs such as the closing of a mine where expenses such as environmental rehabilitation, redundancies and retraining for workers may need to be provided for.

What we will not typically see are any provisions for the externalities outlined above by Kate Raworth. Pavan Sukhdev in his book, 'Corporation 2020',[5] does talk about the development of some appropriate accounting standards for these externalities and goes on to suggest a profit and loss, and Balance sheet, based on these to be read alongside the traditional accounts. I'm not aware of such a practice becoming widespread, much less required by legislation in any major economy.

Genuinely doing this kind of holistic accounting may well reveal the real costs of some industries that we take for granted. At the same time, it may have us all asking what we are prepared to pay for some of the goods we currently regard as cheap. What would happen for example, if the petrochemical industry decided that the costs of removing plastics (including micro plastics) from our oceans

---

5. Pavan Sukhdev, *Corporation 2020* (London: Island Press, 2012).

and waterways should be passed on to the consumer? Every product containing or packaged in plastic would increase dramatically in price. Obviously, they are not the only industry that would have a very expensive shift in the cost of production. The fossil fuel industry, some agribusiness industries faced with the real environmental costs of water, fertiliser, and species loss due to monoculture, could also be in for a tough time. No doubt there are more examples. Even some service industries may need to make some changes because they also use products that are not at this stage fully accounted for in terms of supply chain pollution or in some cases human rights violations and unsafe working conditions. Shifting to a genuinely ecological system of accounting which recognises both ecological costs and benefits, and is fair, will not be easy.

Rising inequality

In her fifth chapter, headed 'Design to Distribute', Kate Raworth deals with rising economic inequality. She begins the chapter by pointing out this economic inequality is no longer about rich nations, middle income developing countries and poor nations, but is clearly impacting nearly all nations internally. Asking about where the millions of poor people who lack many of the basics live Kate comments,

> 20 years ago, the answer was easy to guess: almost all of them lived in the world's poorest countries, classified by the World Bank as low-income, with a GDP per person of less than $1000 per year. As a result, tackling global poverty was seen to be a matter of channelling global aid transfers to provide basic public services and stimulate economic growth in those low-income countries. But today, the answer has changed and at first it seems counter-intuitive three quarters of the world's poorest people now live in middle-income countries. Not because they have moved but because their nations have become better off overall and so have been reclassified by the World Bank as middle-income. Many of these countries, however—including the largest such as China, India, Indonesia, and Nigeria—are becoming more unequal, which explains how they can simultaneously be home to most of the world's poorest people.

Wide inequalities lead to poverty in high income countries too, where the gap between rich and poor is now at its highest level for 30 years, leaving a striking number of people short of their essential needs.[6]

This trend is also present here in Australia. Just a couple of decades ago we used to think of the poor as those people who to some extent relied on some sort of welfare payments, with the occasional bit of help from charities, in order to get by. But now many charities are finding that many of their clients are people in full time work but at the lower end in terms of pay rates. Poverty needs to be thought about differently. Essential needs must be covered and, I suggest a small surplus to needs allowed, to enable people to feel a part of society to which they can make a contribution without constantly feeling under financial stress. This indicates a need for a social minimum that is significantly higher than the current unemployment rate.

This current working poor issue is affecting people in critical industries, particularly the caring industries. In these industries a high proportion of workers are female, thus creating an intensified gender equity issue as well. And what does it say about our society when it is the people we ask to educate and care for the very young, those who are less able and the very old are generally the least well paid? Are young children, less able people and the old just an expensive burden on the budget while it is also ok to give tax cuts to the wealthier end of town? Such rising inequality is not a good trend for any society.

A few pages later Kate Raworth tells us about something called the 'Kusnets Curve' first presented in 1955.

> His underlying message—that rising inequality is inevitable stage on the journey towards economic success for all—was too good a story to doubt. The image that Kusnets had already sketched in every economist's mind was soon drawn onto the economists' page and named the 'Kusnets curve'. With income per person on the X axis and the measure of national income inequality on the Y axis, the curve—shaped like an upside-down U—appeared to present an economic law of motion. And it whispered a powerful message: if you want progress, inequality is inevitable. It's got to get worse before it can get better, and growth will make it better.[7]

---

6. Raworth, *Doughnut Economics*, 164–165.
7. Raworth, *Doughnut Economics*, 167.

Kate goes on to tell us that this inverted U curve rapidly became popular with policy makers around the world and in the world of development economics began to be used as basic theory;

> where it bolstered the theory that poor countries should concentrate income in the hands of the wealthy since only they could save and invest enough of it to kick-start GDP growth.[8]

W. Arthur Lewis who was a leading economist in this approach to being proactive in helping poor nations to find a way out of poverty, and Kuznets both received a noble prise for this highly popular theory. However, as Kate Raworth points out, the data on which this theory was worked out coincided with an unusual period of history. Kuznets' data came from the UK, USA and Germany over the period from 1920(possibly including some data from just before World War I) to 1955. This period includes two very expensive wars and the boom and bust of Wall Street crash and great depression. These events were hugely destructive of personal and corporate wealth. To get economies working again during the Great depression saw huge investment, not by individuals and corporations but by governments. Such government spending by its nature has a far broader impact across the population than is typical of private investment. Then came World War II, enormously more expensive than WW I. After that came the reconstruction of western Europe and Japan, largely funded under the Marshall plan by the USA. Yet more huge government funding was involved. At the same time World War II was massively destructive of private wealth in Europe and East Asia.

Private wealth is what we see at the top end of social inequality. Where does this come from? Recalling what was said earlier about company profits as being the difference between income and expenses, providing that income is the larger figure, we end up with a surplus. Something similar can be the case for individuals and households. For example, if a family's income is sufficient to cover all the basics of the cost of living with a surplus left over, say about $500 a fortnight on average then a surplus is being created. This could be used in a couple of ways. It could be spent on what is called discretionary spending. This means buying goods or services that you would like but don't

---

8. Raworth, *Doughnut Economics*, 167.

really need, a night on the town or that really cool jacket you saw in a shop window. But these ongoing surpluses could be saved until there is enough to buy income producing assets, shares and or property. For as little as $2000 a marketable parcel of shares in a listed company can be bought. Doing this over a couple of years on a savings rate of $500 a fortnight could likely see a thirty-to-forty-thousand-dollar diversified portfolio of listed shares.

This not intended as financial advice. Rather as a way underling a critical point in our current mainstream economic system. In households that seem to have little chance at ever achieving consistent surpluses, no matter how small, are going to be stuck right where they are', or if there is any sort of economic shock, be thrown into poverty in relation to the rest of the society in which they live. In our current economic system, there exists a bias whereby wealth attracts more wealth and, in the process, creates social inequity while fostering hierarchical societies were power and wealth are held in the hands of a few.

This application of surplus income, as a means to growing wealth, for individuals, families and corporations, has become easier to do for those who already have considerable wealth over the last few decades. In the 1980's neo-liberal politicians began to really push policies based on Kuznets' upside-down U curve. In particular under Margret Thatcher in the UK and Ronald Regan in the USA. They were convinced that governments were not the best managers of a range of public utilities and services so sold off potentially profitable government enterprises to reduce debt and, more crucially, cut corporate and private income taxes in ways that favoured high earners most. If personal taxation based on income is seen to be a method of redistributing wealth it doesn't seem to work very well. The data on wealth inequality shows that it actually has the opposite effect. If we want to 'Design to Distribute' as Kate Raworth suggests then we need to think about ways to prevent the accumulation of wealth in the hands of the few at the top of the economic tree.

To some extent this was done up until the mid-twentieth century. When I was a small child, we lived on a small mixed farm. Talking with my mother about this time, she once told me that my father had taken out probate insurance just a couple of months before his sudden death. This was the reason why we had been able to keep the farm for a time rather than being forced into a sale following his death. Such 'death taxes' were not very popular, and if poorly designed they could put 'asset rich but cash poor people' like my mother in awkward situations. However, looking for ways to prevent the intergenerational growth of large fortunes may be a good idea when considering the 'Design to Distribute' theme as a way of countering growing inequality.

In this chapter we have only touched on some of the seven themes of 'Doughnut Economics', represented by the chapter titles and subtitles. We have spent more time with Kate Raworth's critique of the prevailing neo-liberal story than with her creative solutions. What has become clear is that making a significant shift in the world economy that helps us to deal with climate change and the related challenges of the other externalities human civilisation faces on planet earth is not going to be easy. The transformative vision that is presented by 'Doughnut Economics' may take decades to replace the current neo-liberal vision. Part of the problem here is the powerful inertia of the current system. There are many people, particularly those who have profited from it to become wealthy, who will resist many of the changes required. The level of reform required will frighten many voters and politicians.

Resilience

Brian Walker begins the second chapter of his book, 'Finding Resilience', by writing,

> Around 4700 years ago, Gilgamesh, the fifth ruler of the city-kingdom of Uruk in southern Mesopotamia, had some big tree felling plans. He needed timber for ambitious developments in his kingdom—the original go-for-growth policy—and he began felling the cedar forest of southern Mesopotamia.[9]

Gilgamesh might be the first documented 'go-for-growth' leader, but there is archaeological evidence that irrigated farming began some 5000 years earlier in various parts of the world, enabling the accumulation surplus food and seasonal labour to build monuments. Mainstream civilisation, it seems, began to emerge soon after the advent of the Holocene, largely in major river valleys. Those rivers

---

9. Brian Walker, *Finding Resilience* (Clayton South: CSIRO Publishing, 2019), 13.

flowing from high mountain ranges across dryer temperate zones. (Nile, Euphrates, Tigris, Indus, Ganges and Yangtse.) Snow and glacier melt increased the reliability and strength of flow in these river systems. This led to multiple crops becoming possible each year. Significant surpluses meant far more than mere survival had become possible.

This dynamic of concentration of wealth and power in specific locations led to the development of social hierarchies. We see this in political and military institutions with kings and nobility running the show. It is also present in religious institutions with dedicated priesthoods and temple/ monument building etc. Here we have the emergence of empire, which is still very evident today where economic growth is the main goal, bringing with it inequality and social inequity.

During the Holocene getting—away with this kind of empire civilisation may have been ok in a limited way, but as a global norm, has led us into the Anthropocene: an altogether more dangerous situation that can only get worse if we stick with "business as usual".

It is in this context that Brian Walker writes his book on resilience. In the second chapter of his book Brian seeks to define the meaning of resilience. He writes,

> The word resilience is now commonplace in ecology, psychology, sociology, engineering urban development, agriculture, industry, even as a personal philosophy. And in all of them it is used in a somewhat different ways, thereby running the danger of becoming meaningless jargon. This would be most unfortunate because, if we are to successfully navigate the very real and dangerous global trends, it is resilience that needs to be understood and fostered . . . resilience is often referred to as the ability 'to bounce back', but it is not about bouncing back. It is the ability to absorb a disturbance and in the process re-organise so that the system (whatever it is) stays much the same kind of system: not exactly, but functioning in the same way, retaining its identity. It doesn't go back to just how it was. It 'learns' from the disturbance by altering the amounts of its different parts and the relations between them, and so makes it better able to deal with such a disturbance in the future.[10]

---

10. Walker, *Finding Resilience*, 15.

Accepting this definition of resilience gets us closer to successfully dealing with change. It means that seeking to simply go back to the way it was before disturbance is not an option. During the recent covid 19 pandemic we often heard the phrase 'I'll be glad to get back to normal' with little awareness that this was not what was likely to happen. During the pandemic the focus was on taking various actions to control it spread while working on immunisation. This effort involved the closing of borders, lockdowns, emergency social restrictions, various governments pouring money into national economies in ways that were often not well targeted, and a drastic reduction in international travel and trade. At the same time, we had an escalation of conflict between Russia and the Ukraine. We also began to see as commonplace an ongoing climate induced series of major weather events. It now seems that somewhere in the world people are experiencing, record heatwaves, fires, droughts and floods. This is only a summary of shocks that the earth and humanity have experienced.

All of these events listed above are shocks to what we used to call normal. They are disturbances which have caused changes to the different parts of human civilisation and the relations between them. Economically, the uneven nature of the restart of international supply chain has resulted in demand outstripping available supply so fuelled unexpected inflation which has been further exacerbated by large increases in oil and gas prices resulting from sanctions against Russia because of the war in Ukraine. There has been a shift from low inflation to high inflation. This is not a wage-price spiral out of the textbook of neo-liberal economics yet central banks have still used higher interest rates combat it. Small business and mortgage borrowers are the ones taking the brunt of this strategy while the big corporations are still making large profits. In previous occasions of rising interest rates many large corporations were heavily geared. Much more of their financing was done with borrowed money than is typical today. The global financial crisis forced a corporate rethink about having a heavy reliance on having too much debt verses share capital. This means that rising interest rates are less effective in reigning in the spending of listed companies. Consequently inequity, both social and financial, is being exacerbated. Did a few central bankers get it wrong? Possibly!

We can see here that Brian Walker's definition of resilience is in play for human civilization. We have had a number of shocks over the past few years, some from climate, some from adverse human actions and the pandemic. The world we are living in is different and for many more difficult. The burden of the changes between the parts and the relations among them has on the whole, fallen on the world's poor and disadvantaged. The winners have largely been those that had already had considerable wealth. In response to this increasing number of shocks we still do not see any serious challenge to the underlying drivers of our human civilisation. The prevailing mainstream economic system, national sovereignty, international relations and the aspirations of individuals and families for greater material standards of living remain. In that sense the identity of our civilisation is still intact, it is still functioning pretty much the same way. We are not yet starting to develop a different way of going about the business of human civilisation in more sustainable manner. We are not any closer to being in Kate Raworth's doughnut as the safe space for humanity. We are not yet thinking of relational wealth as a completely different worthwhile measure of a successful life. Our global Identity as a civilisation is still the one that started in ancient Mesopotamia in the early Holocene. As the planet warms more increasing shocks await us. If anything, the situation is continuing to get worse and most of us continue to resist change and to hope for some technological silver bullet.

The history of human civilisations from the middle of the Holocene up to the present is often described as the rise and fall of various civilisations. Sometimes this involves competition between different centres of power within a region. This competition can be violent, directed towards the defeat of a rival and the taking over the lands, population and wealth previously ruled by the defeated rival. And so, one civilisation falls and another rises. At other times the fall of a civilisation can be the result of resource exhaustion, such as deforestation or loss of soil fertility and reduced food security.

Today's global civilisation is very likely reaching the limits of the earth's regenerative ability. We may well have passed such limits already. Competition between independent nation states, particularly between major powers and economies, puts further pressure on global civilisation. Pulling against each other may also lead to a collapse of civilisation. Alexander's conquest of the Persian empire is an example of this. He died young, before a consolidated administration of his vast new empire could be enacted. Instead, his three senior generals decided to split it between them. It did not last. Three centuries later the rising power of the Roman empire absorbed the western Greek kingdoms and eastern provinces became the short-lived Parthian empire. Four centuries later the Roman empire in the west also collapsed leaving a smaller eastern end known as the Byzantine empire, centred on modern Turkia.

Over the next decades we may see a collapse of our current global civilisation if it can't be transformed into something much more sustainable. Brian Walker's definition of a resilient system was about a system's ability to be changed by various shocks without losing it identity. In the case of our current system of global civilisation it is too late to shore up its resilience such that it retains its identity. This would simply make matters worse. Human civilisation needs to be transformed in ways that give it a new identity. An identity that has long-term sustainability as a core component.

Chapter 3
Indigenous Knowledges

A More Sustainable Way

Indigenous knowledges are frequently cited as being important with respect of climate change and ecological understanding. However, what is being stated here is frequently not being explained clearly. Non-indigenous people are often left thinking that this is only about particular land management techniques that might become useful as a part of the kitbag of techniques for managing changes in the ecology. For example, a way of managing fuel loads in forests to mitigate future spread and intensity of wildfires. What is not often thought of is the capacity of indigenous knowledge to help build a different civilisation that is fundamentally more sustainable than the one, we have now.

In recent years a new series of books called 'First Knowledges,' edited by Margo Neale has begun to appear. So far six volumes have been published with three more planned. The six books so far published include, 'Songlines' by Margo Neale and Lynne Kelly (2020), 'Design' by Alison Page and Paul Memmott(2021), 'Country' by Bill Gammage and Bruce Pascoe (2021), 'Astronomy' by Karlie Noon and Krystal De Napoli (2022), 'Plants' by Zena Cumpston, Michael-Shawn Fletcher and Lesley Head (2022), and 'Law' by Marcia Langton and Aaron Corn (2023). 'Innovation', 'Medicine' and 'Seasons' are yet to come. Great care has been taken in the publication of this series to check that the information that is shared is of a public nature and not material that may be culturally restricted. While there have been many more books published on aspects of Aboriginal culture, knowledge and history this series brings together a holistic picture of the complexity and depth of Aboriginal civilisation in pre-colonial Australia.

In this chapter we will focus on the sixth book in the series, 'Law', because it is law that connects all the various knowledges together and reveals many of the underlying themes and principles that underpin aboriginal civilisation.

Marcia Langton and Aaron Corn in their book, *Law*, in the chapter titled, 'First Law', have this to say,

> All human cultures have systems of law designed to help societies function and maintain standards of living. Ancient sites and artefacts show us that humans have lived in Australia for at least 65,000 years, which pre-dates the human settlement of Europe and the Americas. Over this immense stretch of time, Indigenous groups across Australia developed complex systems of law that enabled people to live in a wide variety of natural environments and changing climatic conditions. Indigenous systems of law carry countless generations of knowledge. Without law, the ancestors who arrived, travelled and created human societies here would not have survived and thrived over more than sixty-five millennia. These changed over time but were able to continue through major climatic changes, such as the last Ice Age peak around 20,000 years ago and the last major sea-level rise some 10,000 years ago.
>
> Human history in Australia then, began more than 65,000 years before the British started to colonise this continent in 1788. Over those long millennia, Indigenous peoples of Australia came to value the keeping of law as the most significant endeavour in life. Following law in Indigenous societies is the most important and time-honoured way of living. Through law, people express their humanity, honour their ancestors, care for their homelands and environments, understand the past and present, build families and communities, grow in wisdom, and plan for the future[1]

Marcia and Aaron also remind us that,

> Today, however, indigenous systems of law in Australia are vulnerable. They are at risk of being overwhelmed entirely by Crown law—especially the criminal justice system—and competing economic priorities. Yet it is important to

---

1. Marcia Langton & Aaron Corn, *Law* (Port Melbourne: Thames & Hudson, 2023), 35.

remember that these systems of law were developed over many millennia and are tied inextricably to the original ancestors who shaped Australia and birthed its Indigenous people. This precious legacy deserves to survive, because its life-giving and life-affirming gifts can teach us all about how to live in Australia and the rest of the world and adapt to the critical challenges of our age.[2]

Kate Raworth in the first chapter, *Change the Goal*, of her book on *Doughnut Economics*, provides a graph that shows variations in the earth's surface temperature over the past hundred thousand years derived from Greenland ice cores.[3] She uses this to emphasize the unusual stability of the Holocene period in relation to the previous ninety thousand years. That is the period we refer to as the ice ages. It is generally recognised that the climate during that time would have been both dryer and colder than that of the Holocene. Because the graph doesn't show actual temperatures, I got the ruler out to try and get a sense of the amplitude of variation between the two eras. I came up with about 3mm for the Holocene and about 21mm for the ice age. That gives an instability about seven times greater during the previous ninety thousand years, during which Aboriginal civilisation was developing in Australia for at least fifty thousand years.

Australia has always been a continent with a difficult climate. Situated on the southern hemisphere's desert belt most of it is arid or semi-arid. It also has a tropical north subject to summer monsoonal rains and tropical cyclones. It is also known as a land of frequent droughts and flooding rains, influenced by the El Niño-Southern Oscillation. Which describes the cycle of El Niño, neutral and La Niña patterns in the Pacific Ocean, which occur on time scales of typically three to seven years. El Niños often lead to drier conditions over large parts of Australia, while La Niñas tend to enhance rainfall over much of the continent. It is worth noting that this three to seven-year cycle is not a seasonal thing but impacts all seasons throughout the year. This has been a feature of Australia's climate for the Holocene. With global warming it has begun to intensify.

When these climatic issues are considered, Australia has been and continues to be perhaps the least conducive continent (with the

---
2. Langton & Corn, *Law*, 61.
3. Raworth, *Doughnut Economics*, 47.

exception of Antarctica) for human habitation. It is in this context that Aboriginal civilisation has evolved and endured for longer than any other human society, or civilisation. Underpinning this is Law in its aboriginal form. Marcia and Aaron explain that,

> In indigenous languages of Australia common words for law mean precisely what they mean in English and more. Fundamentally, law is a system of rules created an observed within societies to instil people with good values and encourage beneficial behaviours. However, common words for law in indigenous languages such as *rom* in the Yolnu languages, hold broader meanings and 'law' does in English. The idea of law in Indigenous societies, while remaining a system of rules for social good, also includes the idea of English word 'culture'. Beyond this, it also captures the idea of 'proper practise'—the correct way of living a good life, as passed down from the ancestors over many generations—and the idea of 'the way': the path through life shown by ancestors who have gone before . . . Keeping law is about more than just following rules—it is a way of living that honours the sacred relationships Indigenous people hold with their ancestors and homelands . . . Law sets it's a basic standard for acceptable behaviours in Indigenous societies, as well as high learning standards for educating leaders in society. When law functions properly, it creates optimal conditions for maintaining peace and stability.[4]

The inclusiveness of the idea of law presented here with its extension to culture, spirituality, education and respectful behaviour allow it to be seen as an underlying philosophical basis for an enduring civilisation. One of the key concepts in this philosophy is the understanding that everything is related. In Indigenous ways of knowledge, the focus is always on the relationships between various things rather than focus on specific elements. There is no siloing of different fields of knowledge, or separation of academic disciplines that is so common in western society. The indigenous focus on relationships leads to a much more holistic vision of the world. In their chapter headed 'Everything is Related', Marcia and Aaron talk about the Warlipiri people of the Tanami Desert and in particular

---

4. Langton & Corn, *Law,* 35–37.

the work of the late, great artist Kumantye Jakamara and his painting called, 'Possum and Wallaby Dreaming'. This 1985 painting was incorporated into the forecourt Australia's new parliament house as a giant mosaic on an island within a pool, under licence. The artwork is a depiction of the Jardiwarnpa ceremony, which is an annual public ceremony where the whole community participate. It is a purification ceremony performed each year in which all disagreements, enmities and hostilities are laid to rest. This is the first of a cycle of four main ceremonies performed thought the year. Each of these is led by one of the four groups that form Warlipiri society.

> all four main groups are equal and responsible to each other under law. All four groups have senior elders qualified and authorised through the formal learning processes of the annual ceremonial cycle to negotiate agreements and make decisions on behalf of their groups, but these agreements and decisions must also be confirmed by the other three groups, whose views carry equal weight. Because all four groups are closely related through family structures, each has a vested interest in delivering good outcomes for all. That each group also holds responsibility for each producing different parts of the four main annual ceremonies serves to assure their cooperation even further. Overall, this system, as founded by the original ancestors, is designed to ensure that no one group or family lineage can dominate the whole of society, and the needs of all are continually negotiated and balanced to provide the best possible social outcomes. This is the principal way that balance of power is maintained among different groups in Warlpiri society.[5]

When one looks at Kumantye Jakamara's Possum and Wallaby dreaming painting one element that can be seen is the use of four different colours to represent the estates of the four groups in Warlpiri society. The groups are called *Wanya-parnta* (Emu—blue, depicting water), *Parra* (Day—green, depicting vegitation), *Wawirri* (Red Kangaroo—red, depicting blood) and *Munga* (Night—yellow, depicting stars).[6] The four-colour pattern indicates which group holds these different homelands. What is remarkable here is that we

---

5. Langton & Corn, *Law*, 69.
6. Langton & Corn, *Law*, 66.

are not looking at four defined territories as we might expect form a mainstream viewpoint. Instead we find a patchwork of about 160 distinguishable estates. About forty for each group spread across the entire extent of Warlpiri country. This results in what we might call economic equity between the groups.

In arid and semi-arid environments, like the Tanami Desert, the carrying capacity of the land may vary considerably, both in terms of seasonal variation and climate variability form year to year. What this complex arrangement of estates provides for each group, is a distribution of estates granting resources of near equal total value. In this way resources and responsibilities remain on a long-term equitable basis.

These four main groups in Warlpiri society are classified by anthropologists as *patri-semimoieties*, meaning that kinship follows the male line. This means that an individual shares a group or moiety, with their father but must marry outside that moiety. This ensures that the individual will have a grandparent from each of the four groups. These kinship relationships help to strengthen group relationships with each other and thus the whole functioning of the broader society is strengthened. The term moiety basically means that there are two main discernible groups, which may have sub sections, in a society which determine kinship relations. There are various different forms of this moiety type of kinship social relations across Australia. What is common to them all is the way they strengthen and support the overall cohesion of aboriginal society and law.

Every society requires leadership if it is to be well governed. Marcia and Aaron's chapter on leadership is actually entitled 'Wisdom and Leadership'. This title gives an important clue as to how leaders are chosen and developed. Knowledge and wisdom are critical for good leadership. Marcia and Aaron go on to explain how the process of the four major annual ceremonies of the Warlpiri constitutes a twelve-stage formal education system. Each of these levels are more challenging the previous ones.

> Children are traditionally introduced to ceremonial life through the public context of the Jardiwarnpa, which they must attend three times to complete grades 1-3. Males, for example, are then initiated into young adult responsibilities at puberty through grades 4-6 in the seclusion of the Kurdiji ceremony. More advanced learning is undertaken through

grades 7-9, in the seclusion of the can Kankarlu ceremony. The three final grades, reinforce previous learnings in the secluded Kurdiji ceremony are designed to train *yuwarlpiri* (people keepers)—fully knowledgeable and authorised Warlpiri leaders.[7]

Alongside this formal grade education processes a great deal of less formal learning will be going on in the midst of day-to-day life. There will be learning about social norms and respect for others, particularly towards more senior people. There will be learning about the skills required to live successfully on county. The foremost teacher of the people is always country itself. At the same time current leaders will be observing behaviours and personality traits of those progressing through both forms of learning, and so discerning who might be encouraged to take on the challenges of the final three stages.

It is interesting to note what is not present in traditional aboriginal society and that which is specifically avoided. Leadership in aboriginal societies is not something that can be inherited from father to son, or mother to daughter, which is often the model in the history of western, or mainstream societies. Nor is leadership something that can simply be left to chance or emerge from some sort of contest for power. Such power often emerging from the accumulation of surplus resources in the hands of liner families past down directly from parents to children so that sons, or daughters can inherit not only wealth generated by previous generations of the same family but also the social status and political power of that family regardless of their ability to be wise leaders. Rather leadership in aboriginal societies is something that is a result of a deliberate process of education and developed through the discernment of current leaders.

We noted earlier that social and economic equity is maintained through the double moiety system of kinship relationships across four main groups in Warlpiri society where important decisions made by leaders must be supported by leaders from all the groups. This amounts to decision making where it is important to establish a consensus among the leadership group. This enables the society to move forward together. Being able to move forward together is a very important quality for sustainability in what is often a difficult environment.

---

7. Langton & Corn, *Law,* 160.

Earlier when discussing the multiple Warlpiri estates, or homelands, we noted the fairness in the way they are distributed across the broader Warlpiri lands. What is not present when we consider these estates is any notion that they can be alienated as property that can be bought and sold. In that sense they are not held on the basis of freehold title in the sense that mainstream society operates where land can be bought and sold. These estates are held on the basis ancestral relationships. The original creation/first ancestor beings that first brought life to these estates continue to both bring life to them and their descendants. To alienate them through the buying and selling of land would disinherit following generations of the people thus making them homeless. This simply cannot be done lest the whole society fall apart.

If we are wanting to enhance the relationship between people and country/land as an approach to a more sustainable civilisation, then one key question surrounds how we treat the land on which we live. How might we not treat land as a tradeable commodity and prevent it from becoming a wealth creation asset? During the Covid 19 pandemic one of the unintended consequences of the massive amount of government money that was pumped into the economy was a boom in land prices. Before the pandemic we were living on a property that was valued between $500,000 to $600,000. By the end of the pandemic the valuation was more like $1,000,000 without us doing anything. Of course, this was happening all around so we couldn't cash in and buy something better. It has however had a detrimental effect on those who did not already own property. We also need to remember that the house we live in is not generally an income producing asset and may well become the most expensive consumer purchase we ever make.

Owning a house in Australia has become the main method of obtaining long term security of housing. Unlike some other western societies housing is not normally available on long term leases. One-year leases, needing renegotiation, are typical and these favour investors who may wish to sell when the market is high.

Might we consider lifetime leases for the land while allowing the value of built infrastructure to be bought and sold as a better model than freehold title? Such leases would last until the occupier died or decided to move for any reason. Then the new occupants would be given a new lifetime lease. Ideas of this kind would reduce the commodification of land and allow us to be more respectful of the country on which we live. This is something to look at.

Conclusions for Part One

In this first part on climate change, we have looked at in and around the issue of living with a changing climate. We started with trying to get a handle on the complexity of the issue. In particular we noted that the term has become shorthand for a variety of externalities that interact with each other. It is not just about an energy transition away from carbon. We also tried to get a sense of the current state of play. We also noted that issues around national sovereignty and particular national interests make a co-ordinated global strategy difficult. A look at technological approaches to the task and found that while some significant progress is being made, there are still many promising technologies that have still to work through the pilot and scaling up stage. In an attempt at realism, we arrived at an understanding that getting to carbon neutral may well take longer than we expect. Next, we noted that there are still many popular aspirations around improvements in material lifestyles that tend to fuel the very over consumption that has led us into this crisis. There is a great need to change hearts and minds at the grass roots level. This will be a multi-generational crisis.

In Chapter 2 we spent time looking at economics and resilience. Kate Raworth's Doughnut economics seeks to change the goal of economics from is current goal of endless economic growth to one that seeks to create a long-term safe place for humanity within the doughnut. This is about transformative change and actually opposes the resilience of the current system. Kate is talking about changing the identity of the system not making it more resilient. The close connection between economics and the governance, from local to international, of our current civilisation means that human civilisation requires transformative change such that it gains a new identity. This is sounding like the opposite of what Brian Walker is talking about with wanting to enhance the resilience of ecosystems that are under pressure from human activity. But is this so? Can both be done side by side? I think so.

In this chapter we have spent some time looking into the way the world's oldest and most enduring civilisation managed to do this in response to one of the world's most challenging environments. The focus was on governance, high quality leadership, and the importance of relational awareness such that the wellbeing of both the environment and the human community were enhanced. In part this was achieved through environmental management that made resources needed by the community both more abundant and more easily accessible.[8]

As a part of trying to improve the ecological diversity and resilience of the land we live on we planted a wide range of different trees and shrub. This was done on the basis that ecological complexity is a good thing. Not everything has done well, but some trees and shrubs have done well in the conditions. Of note are two varieties of small tree. One is the hakea wattle, a native of the arid area on mainland Australia, making it very drought tolerant. Here in one of dryer valleys of Tasmania it seems to grow well as a result of the slightly damper conditions. The other is the Morrisby gum, an endangered species, whose normal range is closer to the sea where conditions are less subject to frost. Both are thriving here, perhaps because the climate is a bit warmer than it once was. I have also successfully propagated both from seed. These are small examples of human management that have shifted tree species in a way that preserve them for a slightly different ecology in response to climate change. This is a small thing and I'm sure many another gardener has done something like this. It is simply one small way of adaptation to a new reality.

In making these small adaptations through focusing on the environment, both ecological and social, we begin shaping ourselves for a new way of living on planet earth. In this process we become different to what we were, subtle step by step. We discover ourselves being changed in our hearts and minds.

This thought leads us towards the next two parts of this book. The next part focuses on the theology and spirituality of my ancestors in part two in preparation to wrestling with an appropriate Christian theology for the coming age.

---

8. If the reader is interested in learning more about this the third book in the First Knowledges series, *Country*, by Bruce Pascoe and Bill Gamage and also Bruce Pascoe's *Dark Emu*, (Broome: Magabula Books, 2014), and Bill Gamage's, *The Biggest Estate on Earth*, (Crows Nest: Allen and Unwin, 2011).

Part 2 Invasion and Response—Woorrady

Chapter 4
Exploring the theology of Woorrady

Epistemological Issues

At the heart of this exploration of Woorrady's theology there are epistemological and hermeneutical issues that we need to be aware of. The texts that we will be examining are extracted from NJB Plomley's monumental editing works on the Journals of George Augustus Robinson and surviving records pertaining to the Wybelena Mission on Flinders Island.[1] First, there is a need to recognise that Woorrady did not write these stories down and certainly not in his native language. The English in which he told the stories was not on a first language basis. Secondly, the writing down of these stories was by educated Englishmen for their own purposes. This means that the records we have to work with are often not full transcripts of what Woorrady actually said. Sometimes they are close to this but more frequently they are just 'jog the memory notes' for later report writing if needed. Despite these problems we are left with having to take these stories at face value and apply what may seem to some, far too much creative theological imagination.

I have wrestled with these stories now for over a decade. In that time, I have also tried to write about them several times and failed to do them justice. It is in this context that the realisation has dawned on me that a different approach is needed. In my youth I was privileged to have an extensive university education in philosophy and theology across three degrees, including post graduate research, in the western tradition. Using some categories of interpretation that come out of

---

1. NJB Plomley, *Friendly Mission 2nd edition* (Hobart:Quintus Publishing, 2008) and *Weep in Silence* (Hobart: Blubber Head Press, 1987)

that education were possibly taking me in unhelpful directions when trying to understand the thinking of a traditional Aboriginal man raised in a pre-colonial way.

Spending a decade or so working with increasing focus on trying to live in a twenty-first century way on country/land, since we bought the block here near Kutalayna, seems to have given me a second education. This time in the 'University of Country/land' enabling me to think much more in Aboriginal ways of knowing. Ways of knowledge described by Tyson Yunkaporta, in his book, Sand talk, in the chapter headed, 'Displaced Apostrophes'.

> In Aboriginal worldviews, nothing exists outside of a relationship to something else. There are no isolated variables—every element must be considered in relation to the other elements and the context. Areas of knowledge are integrated, not separated.[2]

The intense focus on learning to love the country/land I am on has been transformative and instrumental in reshaping both my sense of identity and my spiritual perspective. I have become both stronger and wiser; more able to enter into the worldview of Woorrady. It has done this almost without conscious realisation. The magnitude of change in my sense of self and identity has been huge. It has been literally life changing.

I want to remind you of the story from my childhood about the lamb earlier. That story will help us in understanding how this walking in two cultures can illuminate what is going on in these creation stories. It is the winter 1961 I am four years old, and my brother is five. We are both out on the farm with our father. We're going round the sheep in order to check on the ewes who are about to give birth. My father calls us over to an ewe who is lying on the ground. My brother rushes straight over. I on the other hand have been distracted by something I've seen in the sky. I have seen light coming through the clouds in just that kind of way epiphany stories in my children's Bible picture God speaking from heaven. So, I get there just a bit late to see the whole process of the birth of the lamb. My brother tells me that I've missed it. I deny this and say I saw the lamb coming down from heaven. Perhaps our father could see a potential dispute

---

2. Tyson Yunkaporta, *Sand Talk* (Melbourne: Text Publishing, 2019), 169–170.

between these two boys because he does not try to adjudicate the different perspectives here but rather affirms the validity of both.

This seems to a fairly, simple story. This kind of thing, the birth of a lamb, happens all the time. There is nothing particularly unusual about it. However, there is some complexity in this story. There are at least seven actors in it. There is the ewe and her lamb. The father and his two boys are also there. The creator is also involved. Finally, there is the land/country in terms of the where and when of the action that takes place. What is more there is a complex relational network between all these actors. Western, or mainstream, thinking would home in on the various actors involved. Aboriginal thinking would spot the relational network as the key feature of the story.

If we take the western mainstream approach that focuses on the actors in the story, then some dangers of interpretation become apparent. Some actors may become the focus of interpretation over others. Some being seen as more important than others, allowing a hierarchy to develop. This can happen because of the pre-existing of ideas in the listener as to what is interesting. Many listeners from a mainstream perspective would focus only on the human actors in the story, Setting aside the ewe and the lamb, and also the creator. Alternatively, some deeply religious people may choose to focus on the creator and diminish the others. A biologist, or sheep breeder, might decide to focus on the sheep. Still others might pay attention to all the actors but rank them in order of importance in some way before doing so. The holistic focus may end up being lost altogether and the learning from the story narrowed to just one point of interest.

The Aboriginal approach which begins with the relational network ends up in a very different outcome. The actors are all seen as having a valued place in the story as it would not work without all of them. The father and his two sons have clear relationships to each other, as you would expect. In this story the boys are learners, and their father is teaching them. All three have a significant relationship to both the ewe and the lamb for this is a farming family and the sheep have direct relationship to the family's livelihood. When the Creator is added into this relational network the whole picture opens up into a much bigger story. The father and both his sons, and the ewe and newborn lamb are all related to the creator as creatures. Awareness can then extend, in an open way, to everything else in the environment that surrounds the actors which in an Aboriginal context is country/land.

This simple creation story has a relational openness to country/land and indeed the whole creation and can be valued, inclusive of all its individual actors, as a part of the biggest picture of all.

The reader may have noticed that I frequently refer to country/land. I have chosen to do this in order that it be understood that this is a reference to Aboriginal usage of the word, 'Country'. The English word, country, frequently has other meanings. It can refer to nation states and the territory over which they have sovereignty and so has a geopolitical meaning. It also can refer to the landscape as in phrases like, 'good grazing country', 'good farming country', or beautiful country meaning 'scenery'. In Aboriginal usage 'Country' is much more about a connection to, or belonging to, a particular place of special relationship. This relationship is better described as spiritual or even ecological. It also involves a sense of deep time, present reality, and hope for the future. This is often picked up in the phrase, 'always was and always will be'. My use of the two words, country, and land together in this way hopefully enables the reader to begin to get a deeper understanding of the way Aboriginal people are using the word, 'Country'.

Devils, Spirit or being?

While we are looking at our language it is important to also consider the various terms used by Woorrady and Robinson in the conversations recorded in Robinson's journals. In this context, I prefer the term 'creation/ancestor being' when referring to those beings who are otherwise described by Woorrady as devils. The language in which Woorrady tells his stories is English. This however is a limited version of English. Woorrady largely learnt his English from interactions with woodcutters and whalers in his role as a traditional healer. They called him Doctor because of his expertise in this area. His command of English would no doubt have improved during his relationship with Robinson. However, his English would have remained more of the everyday sort. The English word he has taken up through his conversations with Robinson to describe these 'creation/ancestor beings' is 'devils'. This word comes out of Robinson's evangelical missionary theological language.

The version of the Bible that Robinson used and was very familiar with is the authorised or King James version. If one looks at the story of the Gadarene swine (in this version of the Bible) from the Gospel of Mark chapter 5 we find that this story concerns many devils. It's a healing story about a man with a serious mental illness who could be violent and was difficult to restrain. He lived amongst the tombs, in a graveyard. This man also told Jesus that his name was 'Legion' because of the many devils within him. The healing of this man takes the form of the 'many devils' being transferred out of him into a herd of pigs, which promptly run down the hill and drown themselves. I do not know if Robinson had ever told Woorrady this story, but it helps us understand Robinson's choice of the word 'devils' as an English translation for the concept of 'creation/ancestor beings'.

In Robinson's world view, that of the evangelical missionary, any spirituality that was not Christian was automatically of the Devil, consequently evil and dangerous, so should be abandoned and replaced with a proper Christian view as he saw it. It is also clear that when he used this word 'devil', that he had been given, Woorrady tended to give it a positive meaning, as did other Aboriginal people, and not the intensely negative one that Robinson intended. To illustrate this investing the word 'Devil' with opposite meanings it is worth quoting a passage from Robinson's journal dated 7th of December 1831, while in central Tasmania, he is referring to a conversation with Mannalargenna,

> the old chief said that the natives had devils that told them when the white men was coming, that the devil walked about with them and kept watch, that he carried with him a torch but no one could see him. I treated this story of the devil with derision, and told them they ought not to put faith in such nonsense.[3]

Should we choose to retain the word 'devil', in this context, we would forever be having to explain our specific usage over and against the word's common usage.

Why not use the English word spirit? Surely this word does not have the negative connotations that the word devil does. We can talk of good and bad spirits. The word spirit has a long history in many cultures. It is part of the language used when talking about the beliefs of many different religious and philosophical traditions the world

---

3. Plomley, *Friendly Mission*, 577.

over. Here lies the danger. We could find ourselves unintentionally importing ideas from somewhere else into the world of Woorrady and his people.

Of particular concern is the tendency in many cultures to see the spiritual and material as two quite distinct realms. The ancient Greek philosopher, Plato, suggested that the whole of reality could be described by means of a vertical diagram. At the bottom of the diagram was the material realm. Dumb matter, that is, ordinary physical objects, being right at the bottom. Then above that were living things, plants, animals and much everyday activity. Next there is a firm line above which we find the mental spiritual aspects of reality. First comes mental activity especially skills like mathematics and rational thinking. Above this is what Plato described as the really real world of forms and ideas. At the top was the 'form of the good', or the place of perfection. Later this was to become understood as heaven. The key thing with this way of thinking about the world was that firm line between the material and spiritual. This led to the belief that that which was above the line was most important and, as a consequence, the material, that part of the world below the line, was not.

This in turn led to the belief that those things above the line—spiritual things—were eternal and not subject to death and decay in the way that all things below the line, were subject to death and decay. Further this became connected to the idea of eternal souls and such souls were not subject to death and decay. In some cultures, this eternal soul could be subject to either eternal damnation or eternal salvation. In others the eternal soul might migrate up and down an eternal chain of being depending on the quality of life that had been lived. This chain of being might go from plain matter to plants to animals, then up to people and eventually find release by going to heaven or Nirvana or some such other place. But in most of this thinking, wherever there is a firm line or separation between the material and spiritual, there is also a tendency to devalue the material because of its transient nature. The result is that only the eternal is regarded as having lasting value.

Projecting these sorts of ideas about the relation of the spiritual to material into the world view of Woorrady and his people could create some serious distortions. This is why the term "creation/original ancestor being" is to be preferred when speaking of Dromerdeene, Moihernee and his children, and even Wrageowrapper. The word "being" simply means that something is, that it exists. The word creation is simply about the ability to do things, to make things. Thus, the term in full, 'creation/original ancestor being', is much more neutral in this context. The words 'original ancestor" are included here in order the give weight to the way aboriginal people will refer to the creation/being of a particular place as a first or original ancestor of the people connected to that particular place. If this is kept in mind, then for simplicity's sake the phrase 'creation being' will do.

However, it is important not to be too pedantic about this term. In Aboriginal culture these beings can also be thought about as 'ancestor beings/spirits'. This indicates a spiritual link between the creator and the created that also reflects the holistic relationship with country. Every individual creature on country has this ancestral link to a creation being associated with country/land.

There are some alternative ways, if less common ones, of seeing the relationship between the material and the spiritual. One of these comes from the New Testament writer, St Paul. He uses the Greek term, *soma pneumaticon*, usually translated as spiritual body. Here Paul is forcing together the spiritual and material into a single unity. In doing so he is insisting that both are part of the whole, that it is a mistake to separate them. The context in which St Paul introduces this idea is the coming salvation. For him this is not about eternal souls going to heaven but about resurrection. In some sense the whole of what constitutes a human being, including the material body, is taken up in the process of salvation.

In contemporary neuroscience we see something similar happening. The use of scanning technology to observe brain activity in response to stimuli, shows patterns where different parts of the brain consistently respond to specific stimuli. While the connections between brain activity and particular mental states is still not fully understood, there is a profound relationship between the two. One of the assumptions, which becomes relevant here, is the description of human beings as psychosomatic beings. That is, the mental and or spiritual cannot be separated from the material. It is noteworthy that the method used to make this connection between mental and emotional states and brain activity, is observational. Neuroscientists observe that there is a clear relationship between what they see on brain scans and the mental and emotional states of test subjects or patients.

This may be much closer to what is going on in the stories that surround Moihernee and his children. It is well known that Aboriginal, indeed hunter-gatherer societies in general, had highly developed observational skills. These were a survival necessity. People simply had to know the where and when by which both food and toolmaking supplies could be found. All this vital information was learnt by observation. This observational knowledge was accumulated over time from continuous observation and experience of the world around them, of the environment. This accumulated observational knowledge was passed on from generation to generation, growing with time. In the same way the activity of Moihernee, and other creation beings were observed, and stories of these observations were told.

This is not to say that Aboriginal knowledge was simply a massive accumulation of observations. While they may not have been gathered together a systematic theory of everything in a modern mathematical or logical system, they did attempt like all human societies to make sense of their world. The stories of creation beings are part of just this process. However, observation was the natural starting point and so stories are told about the where and when of creation beings in action and so we hear talk about sacred sites.

Some years ago, I was invited to travel with a group to the remote area of the Tarkine coast in Tasmania's far west. The group I was with had the intention of exploring the possibility of setting up a wilderness school. I had not been there before. It is a difficult place to reach. It was a five-hour journey by road then camp overnight, followed by a trip to the river mouth by boat and then a half hour or so walk over a range of hills to a camping place. We spent some days there exploring the local area. It was certainly a beautiful and isolated wild region. The adjective 'pristine' was used a lot in conversations about the state of the environment there. I was not so sure. When I got home, I looked up the description of the area given by Robinson on his first journey up that part of the coast. He had this to say, 'Kangaroo abounds very much in this part of the country, which resembles in appearance a park with extensive grassy hills with honeysuckle trees'[4]

This is not what I saw almost 190 years later. Instead, I saw the narrow coastal plain largely covered in dense scrub and on the hills

---

4. Plomley, *Friendly Mission*, 197.

slightly more inland was button grass studded with many small tea trees and the like. Certainly not open grasslands suitable for kangaroo. So, while the ecology has definitely changed since the time it was managed in Aboriginal ways it was by no means pristine wilderness which had probably not been seen in that area for tens of thousands of years. There were, however, signs of typical West Coast rainforest coming back. In some of the gullies between the hills there were a few young eucalypts which, one would expect, given a few more years, might have grown tall enough to provide a canopy for other rainforest plants.

While exploring this country/land I began to recall some of these stories about Moihernee and all the other 'creation beings' belonging to this country/land. It was then that I noticed some interesting shapes in the rocks poking out of the top of some of the low hills. Strange, craggy faces began to emerge. At a deep emotional level, I was given a sense of awesome latent power brooding in these hills, patiently waiting for an opportunity to break free and transform the land, to re-order country/land.

I took some photos.

Was it just my imagination or was I seeing something more? Could this Tarkine coast experience be giving me some hints about a possible return of Moihernee. I don't really know but I would assert that it could be a possibility.

As we grapple with creation stories in this document, we will need to be aware of these very different ways working with such stories.

Chapter 5
Woorrady's Theology

1838 Sermons

In her article 'Before the Second Reformation' Penny Van Toorn quotes the following passage from Robinson's journal annotations dated 14th of April 1838.[1]

> The white men have killed us all; they shot a great many. We are now only a few people here and we ought to be fond of one another. We ought to love God. God made everything, the salt water, the horse, the bullock, the opossum, the wallaby, the kangaroo and wombat. Love him and you go to him bye and bye.

The full quotation has an additional introductory sentence.

'My brothers, in our own country a long time ago we were a great many men, a great number.'[2]

Van Toorn also tells us that between February and April of 1838 there was a practice of weekly meetings of the Aboriginal Tasmanians at Wybelena on Flinders Island for prayer and instruction. During which senior men would address the community. Robert Clark, the catechist, recorded these 'sermons'. The pattern was for these men to speak in their native language and the lingua franca of the community which was a creole of several Aboriginal languages and simple English. This would then be translated into better English by one of the women who were the better linguists. Even in precolonial

---

1. NJB Plomley, *Weep in Silence* (Sandy Bay: Blubber Head Press, 1987) 733. Penny Van Toorn, 'Before the Second Reformation', SENICA.pdf version.
2. Plomley, *Weep in Silence*, 733

society this was the case as men stayed on the same basic social group and county/land, while women always found themselves in a new community and country/land when married. Being at least bi-lingual was normal for them. A fact that Robinson exploited in his missionary journeys.

This process may not have been necessary in Woorrady's case. He was the speaker on this occasion. He would have known if his translator was not being fair. However, it is also likely that Clark's recording is a synopsis of a speech that may well have been longer for Woorrady was a renowned storyteller and may not have been satisfied with such a brief statement.

Who was this man?

Woorrady was born circa 1790 to the Nuenonne people of Bruny Island. This makes him about thirteen years old at the time of the first settlement at Risdon and only slightly younger at the time of the most recent French scientific expedition to the southeast area; he may well have had direct experience of this as he speaks to Robinson about both the French and the arrival of the first settlement ships.[3] He certainly seems to have known about pre-settlement contacts in the area. A list of some 200 people at the Flinders Island establishment and their ages in 1835 includes only seven people over forty at that time. Woorrady is one of them. While there were some others born before settlement who had died during the intervening years the numbers of aborigines who had grown up in the traditional way without settler disruption would have been very few at the time of these weekly meetings. As such, Woorrady would have been well educated and versed in the storytelling and spirituality of his people.

Woorrady is by this time well-travelled and linguistically competent. Prior to his first meeting with Robinson in 1829 at the Bruny Island Mission Woorrady had travelled on at least one occasion outside of the cultural-linguistic community that he had grown up in. He relates a story of crossing Storm Bay to raid the Pydairrerme with the object of acquiring some of their women and relates some of the things he learnt of their culture. Woorrady would also have had numerous interactions with sealers, whalers, woodcutters, convict

---

3. Plomley. *Friedly Mission*, 408.

hunters and settlers prior to 1829. At the time of the establishment of the Bruny Island mission it is evident that he has little trouble communicating with Robinson or with those at the whaling station. Clearly, he already had a good grasp of practical English.

Two years of travelling almost right round Tasmania with Robinson would have not only greatly improved Woorrady's English but also enabled him to meet with Aboriginal people from virtually all the major cultural/linguistic groups and to learn something of their language, culture, and stories.

The broader historical and theological perspective

Woorrady's life bridges the end of the eighteenth century and the early part of the 19th century. It is important to understand what was going on during this same period in England and Europe. The Industrial revolution was happening. The establishment of colonial empires was continuing at an increasing pace with active competition between European nations in this space. Alongside this the period called the Enlightenment was well and truly underway. This movement Involved the rapid development of science as a way of understanding the world. There were major changes in the way the world was beginning to be understood by philosophers and political thinkers across Europe. Already there had been a move towards constitutional monarchy and political governance in the British Isles. The British American colonies had already broken away from English governance and established a Republic. Revolution had also taken place in France. The first attempt, since Charlemagne, to bring all of Europe under a single administration by Napoleon Bonaparte was well underway at the time of the beginnings of the first British settlement in Tasmania. In fact, the invasion itself was decided upon as a result the global strategic struggle between the French and the English. Despite a general understanding of commonality in European civilization the nation state remained the principal form of sovereign identity in Europe. In this sea of change and political turmoil the British had gained a position of leadership beyond other European powers.

In this context the church and theology were struggling to keep up with the changing world. The church was no longer the unifying institution that it had been in central and Western Europe. The Protestant Reformation had taken place a couple of centuries earlier.

This had led to a significant change in the relationship between church and state. In northern Europe the emergence of protestant churches sponsored by kings and princes increased the independent power of those states. What constraint the church had had on princely power because of the cultural and religious authority of the papacy was now removed. In the rest of Western Europe, where Catholicism was the main form of the church, much of the power in this relationship between church and state had also shifted. Kings and princes had considerably more influence in church and state relations because of the decline of papal power. However, by the eighteenth century in some European nation states the power of monarchs begins to become more limited with the rise and increasing wealth of the middle class and the influence of enlightenment political philosophy. The American and French revolutions are clear signs of this. In Britain during this time, we see the evolution of constitutional monarchy with parliament becoming the main centre of political authority.

Ideas about the nature of God and religion were also changing in intellectual circles. The rise of Deism which understood God in terms of simple monotheism and as the 'unmoved mover'. This God was defined as being basically opposite to the created world. Creation is mortal but God immortal. Creation is finite but God infinite. Suffering happens to creatures, but God cannot suffer, and so on. God's role in this context is simply one of getting creation going then keeping his distance.

At this point it is worth quoting Hans Kung's comment about the impact of Descartes' philosophy from the early seventeenth century.

> With Descartes, European consciousness in a critical development reached an *epochal turning point*. Basic certainty is no longer centred on God, but on man. In other words. The medieval way of reasoning from certainty of God to certainty of the self is replaced by the modern approach: from certainty of the self to certainty of God.
>
> Here is a Copernican turning point—no less important than that relating to earth and sun. Instead of Theocentrism we now have a solidly based anthropocentrism. Man stands at the centre and indeed on his own feet. With the utmost energy, resolution and discipline, Descartes set out methodically from man, from the subject, his freedom, reason, certainty, and

was thus the first person to substantiate philosophically the autonomy of science. He has rightly been called the 'Father of modern philosophy' the Father of modern thought.[4]

What we have here with Descartes is the beginnings of a shift in epistemology. How we know things has shifted from a basis in the authority of received knowledge towards the inner certainty felt by the individual which is reflected on by reason. This process picked up by the emerging new science. Mathematics and critical reasoning become major tools for understanding of the world. At the same time personal religious experience becomes much more important for a religious understanding of reality, diminishing institutional authority in the process. Divergent spaces have begun to open up across a wide variety learning disciplines.

By the end of the eighteenth century the enlightenment process has expanded enormously. Natural science has diverged into several discrete areas. Physics, chemistry medicine, astronomy and botany etc. Political philosophy is underway as well. Rousseau is writing about social contract as a form of consent by the populace for national rulers. Locke is developing a political philosophy based on the separation of powers which will be influential in the development of the United States of American constitution. All of this is being increasingly thought of in ways outside of religion. The secular space is expanding rapidly.

To give an idea of just how fast this change influences to role of religion in society there are a couple of thigs to look at. In 1689 the British parliament passed an act of toleration. This act provided for people who were dissenters from the Established Church of England who could take a simplified oath of allegiance to the Crown and would be able to gather for public worship. This would have included Quakers, Congregationalists, Baptists, and other protestant groups. The other is the USA constitution and it First Amendment, ratified in 1791. This forbids any type of established church at all and permits wider freedom of religion. Governance has become basically secular but can still be influenced by the personal religious beliefs of elected officials.

---

4. Hans Kung, *Does God Exist?* (Oxford: University Press, 1978), 15–16.

However, this religious toleration does not extend to everybody. Most Europeans in the early nineteenth century still considered Christianity, in whatever form, to be the most advanced religion. So Christian missionaries were encouraged to enter newly colonised parts of European empires to convert and civilise new subjects of such empires.

The social space for religion is being reduced to providing moral and ethical values to society. What remains of organised religion is being seen as having a functional value to society, helping to maintain social cohesion. Christianity is not yet being openly attacked by the rise of philosophical atheism. The prevailing form of Christian belief and expression is that of Christian monotheism, although personal faith and questions of salvation (as in the soul going to heaven, or hell) are still strong in popular belief.

At this point it is important to mention the influence of the evangelical reform movement that appeared in Britain the late eighteenth century. This was led by upper-class well-educated people, most famously by William Wilberforce seeking to pass legislation to abolish the slave trade in Britain and her dominions. It also included the Wesley brothers, John and Charles, who were university educated Anglicans. They established an itinerant ministry amongst the large number of workers in the new industrial factories and mines. Many of these workers were poorly paid, worked excessively long hours in unsafe conditions. Their families often lived in crowded and unhealthy slum conditions. Social reform was needed here as well. Trade Unionism eventually emerged. Prison reform was another such social reform issue. Governor Arthur, who was responsible for the setting up of the Wybalenna mission had also experimented with prison reform as part of this evangelical reform agenda. His system for dealing with Van Diemen's Land's large convict population aimed at reforming the convicts over and above punitive punishment-based imprisonment. In setting up the mission, like many of his contemporaries, he would have had social reform in mind with respect to welfare of the Aboriginal people at the mission. Educating them to be 'good Christian citizens of the empire' would have been the goal. We would now recognise this as the beginning of the assimilation policy which was to be practiced openly for the next century and a half with devastating results for Aboriginal culture and language right across the Australian continent.

When Thomas Wilkinson, one of the early catechists at the mission, reported to Governor Arthur that he had translated the first chapter of Genesis into an Aboriginal language he was reprimanded. Arthur insisted that all education, including religious education had to be conducted in English. The reform agenda was set on an assimilationist path.

For most of society people were still working with a more medieval metaphysic; the three-tiered universe. The earth was in the centre with hell below and heaven above. Personal salvation was about making sure you got to go up rather than down when life was over. The role of the cross of Christ was about the forgiveness of sins and the possibility that such forgiveness would open the way to heaven. Alongside this also sat the idea that good works were also important in the context of going to heaven. Despite there being some tension between these two ideas. At Wybalenna this was the theology that was taught. One of the other speakers in the series of sermons in 1838 was Druemerterpunner. He appears to be a frequent speaker as 3 of his sermons are in the collection. It is worth quoting all three.

> . . . hell a bad place that you like to go there, do you? do you like to burn plenty, plenty hungry and plenty sick. No good place that, but God's country a good country. Heaven a fine place you like it. No hunger there, no thirst there, no sick, no bad people. All are good there, you like it. Then learn to be good. You are not like me. I don't tell lies, I don't fight . . . (31/3/1838)[5]

> Put away your wicked corroberrys, put away your bad things, your wicked doings. Why don't you love God? . . . You play too much at marbles, you walk about too much, you don't love Jesus Christ enough like me, I love God, I love Jesus Christ, I will go to heaven when I die, no old men there, all young boys there, no sickness there. God love you. If you are good you go to heaven. Heaven a happy place, good people there. (14/4/1838)[6]

> I say my friends Mr. Clark askem you plenty out of God's book and no other white man ask you anything out of the Bible,

---

5. Plomley, *Weep in Silence*, 733
6. Plomley, *Weep in Silence*, 733

> me hear him a long way. You like Jesus Christ do you not my brothers, Jesus Christ came into the world to save sinners. We die we go to heaven. Good people always KRACKNY [stop] in heaven. Mr Clark tellem you Jesus Christ die, was crucified. He die a little one, not a long one. Then he jumped up and went to heaven. By and bye he bring you and me to heaven if we are good people. (21/4/1838)[7]

The notes around the record of these sermons indicate that not all the sermons were recorded. There were occasions when names were recorded of speakers, but no text is given. The very fact that Druemerterpunner is consistently recorded indicates that his speeches were on the money from the point of view of Chaplin Dove and catechist Clark. This indicates the nature of the theology being taught. It is about personal salvation meaning the opportunity to go to heaven and to avoid hell after death. It is also about good and bad behaviours. Behaving in a way that suits British society is clearly good while behaviour that reflects Aboriginal tradition is regarded as somehow bad. This is also in line with official policy which desires that Christianity should be taught in English.

We turn now to a more detailed examination of Woorrady's theology.

What does the text, the synopsis of Woorrady's sermon tell us?

> My brothers, in our own country a long time ago we were a great many men, a great number. The white men have killed us all; they shot a great many. We are now only a few people here and we ought to be fond of one another. We ought to love God. God made everything, the salt water, the horse, the bullock, the opossum, the wallaby, the kangaroo and wombat. Love him and you go to him bye and bye.[8]

This sermon is unique in that it goes beyond the theology present in the other recorded sermons in at least two points. First it sets the historical context and secondly it is centred on the theology of creation rather than that of individual salvation.

---

7. Plomley, *Weep in Silence*, 734
8. Plomley, *Weep in Silence*, 733

The method of interpretation that was introduced above of seeking out the relational connections between actors rather than a focus on the actors will have to wait a while for this sermon. This is because context and change is the place where the action happens. There is a need to understand the both the historical context and the theological change before we can clearly see relationships between these perspectives, Woorrady, his listeners and readers.

Woorrady begins with the trauma and tragedy resulting from the colonial invasion.

> My brothers, in our own country a long time ago we were a great many men, a great number. The white men have killed us all; they shot a great many. We are now only a few people…[9]

In making this introduction to his sermon Woorrady is bearing witness to what has happened to his people over the past four decades or so. If we were to imagine a formal judicial inquiry into the European invasion of Tasmania, Woorrady would be a key witness whose testimony would cover almost the whole of Tasmania and certainly the whole period from first contact up until the time of this sermon. Not only does Woorrady remember seeing the first ships arrive but has also travelled widely with Robinson around Tasmania. This included the journey into the central highlands to negotiate the surrender of the last group of Aboriginal resistance to end the 'Black War' in 'the settled areas'. This group consisted of only twenty-six people. Woorrady would have met and got to know these people on Flinders Island. He would have been aware of their stories. By this time, he may well have been the only Aboriginal person still alive to have had such an extensive overview of the story of invasion by the British.

Estimates of the precolonial population of Tasmania vary between 3000 and over 20000 people. In the literature the consensus figure is around 6000. At the time of this meeting the Wybalenna community numbers about 100 Aboriginal people. Beyond this group there is but a handful of Aboriginal girls and women living within settler society, mostly on smaller offshore islands, and the Laney family in the far northwest. This dramatic population decline has taken place over little more than 3 decades, half a lifetime. At this time the graveyard

---

9. Plomley, *Weep in Silence*, 733

at the mission has almost as many Aboriginal people in it as are left in the living community. Vulnerability to introduced disease, massive cultural and social disruption and war had reduced perhaps a hundred or so different communities to just one, which was also in decline. Woorrady has been witness to all of this; he knows what he is talking about.

I am aware of no evidence of Woorrady becoming a Christian in the classic sense of conversion. This short quote, or sermon, is the only hint that he may have moved towards acceptance of a Christian way of seeing the world. Christian or not Woorrady, in this short sermon, seems to have been willing to accept that the Christian way maybe the only way forward for the younger generation of his people.

> '. . . we ought to be fond of one another. We ought to love God.'[10]

This younger generation is already significantly different to Woorrady's generation in their understanding of the world. Their world view is less shaped by traditional Aboriginal culture, lifestyle and practice than that of Woorrady's generation and more shaped by the culture of the invading British. Most of these younger people have spent significant time interacting with colonial culture. This has included time in the Orphan School in Hobart where they have learnt to read and write in English and have also been exposed to evangelical Christianity and the Bible.

When discussing the impact of Christianity on this younger generation the historian, Henry Reynolds comments,

> The intriguing point is that the young people who were most influenced by European ideas in general, and Christianity in particular, were the strongest advocates of Aboriginal rights. In the hands of Walter and Mary Arthur, Christianity became a means of shaping and affirming a new Aboriginal identity, and a new sense of political agency. It gave them confidence in dealing with Europeans. They absorbed the essentially egalitarian message of the evangelical Christianity that all people were the children of God—that the most important distinctions were not those between white and black, 'savage' and 'civilised', but between sinners and the saved.[11]

---

10. Plomley, *Weep in Silence*, 733
11. Henry Reynolds, *Fate of a Free People*, (Camberwell: Penguin Books, 2004)172.

Walter George Arthur, Drinene (Neptune), Tillarbunner (John Allen) and along with Woorrady's son, Myyungge (Davey) were the signatories to the petition to Queen Victoria that led to the close of Wybalenna and the return to the Tasmanian mainland.

Of the small group (less than 50) who returned to mainland Tasmania only one had descendants, Fanny Cochrane Smith. Fanny was only a young child, about four years old,[12] at the time of these sermons. She may well have been present but what she took in or how the whole process affected her it is hard to know. She married a white settler and obtained a small land grant at Nichols Rivulet in the south of Tasmania where they farmed and engaged in the timber industry. She later donated a part of this land for the building of a small Methodist Chapel and became a leading figure in that church. Fanny also maintained elements of Aboriginal culture. As an older woman she made recordings, using an early gramophone, of songs she had learnt as a child in Aboriginal language. While Fanny had integrated into mainstream colonial society, she clearly remained a proud Aboriginal person.

Fanny was not the only survivor. The descendants of the 'sealer women' continued as a distinct community in the Bass Strait Islands (and on Kangaroo Island off the South Australian coast). However, they became known officially as Cape Baren Islanders and for over a century were not considered Aboriginal, being of mixed race. There were also mixed-race descendants on mainland Tasmania who had never been to the islands. The most well-known of these being the descendants of Dalrymple Johnson who had entered colonial society as a small child and who was sufficiently well connected to have her mother brought to live with her instead of being held at Wybelena. My own ancestor, Maryanne Coates captured in an undocumented settler raid around 1824 was also never sent to Flinders Island managing to live 'under the radar'. There are also other traditions of Aboriginal decent that are less well documented in the colonial records.

After the death of the last of the survivors from Wybelena officialdom declared that there were no longer any Tasmanian aborigines. This was taught in schools up until the late 1960s. However unofficially in mainstream culture people remembered

---

12. Lyndall Ryan, *Tasmanian Aborigines a history since 1803* (Crows Nest: Allen & Unwin, 2012). Cover portrait information, in the front of Book.

which families had Aboriginal ancestry. Racism was very real for our people. So bad was this that many in the early twentieth century went to considerable effort to 'pass over' by splitting up families and moving away to places where nobody was likely to know the story. If the children looked white enough, then maybe, they could grow up without racism. This happened in my family.

It was not until the 1970s that reassertion of Aboriginal identity and cultural heritage was able to begin in Tasmania, and it has been and continues to be a struggle.

The exile to Flinders Island was ended by the petition to Queen Victoria but in way it marked the beginning of another form of exile. It marked the beginning of the experience of being exiles in our own land.

> God made everything, the salt water, the horse, the bullock, the opossum, the wallaby, the kangaroo and wombat. Love him and you go to him by and bye.[13]

This last part of Woorrady's sermon develops an understanding of God as creator. It is interesting that list of created animals also includes the horse and the bullock; both introduced to Tasmania by European settlers. It seems it is possible that Woorrady is speaking as much to the 'whitefellas' listening in as he is to the Aboriginal audience. In his introduction he has already born witness to the rapid destruction of Aboriginal society in Tasmania by the 'whitefellas'. Now at the end, he is reminding both his Aboriginal audience and the 'whitefellas' that they are all part of the relationship between the Creator and his creation. Is this accommodation or critique?

In answering the above question, it will be important to examine in more detail Aboriginal stories of creation and the history of the conversation between Woorrady and Robinson, on the theme of creation. In particular, the conversations that took place on their trip into the northeast of Tasmania almost a decade earlier.

---

13. Plomley, *Weep in Silence*, 733

Chapter 6
Conversations on the theme of Creation
July 1831

Introduction to the Texts

The text that is quoted below originates from the journal entries dated between the 7th and 12th of July 1831 and if taken from the 'Friendly Mission: The Tasmanian Journals and Papers of George Augustus Robinson 1829–1834' Edited by NJB Plomley, Second Edition, Queen Victoria Museum and Art Gallery and Quintus Publishing, 2008. The page numbers given are from the second edition.

I have chosen to begin the two quotations at the points where Robinson initiates the conversations. In the first and longer quotation Robinson asks a question about the creation of the first people. In the second quotation he initiates the conversation by telling stories from the Book of Genesis. This is done in order to provide some context for the telling of Woorrady's stories. The framework of the conversations is essentially what we might understand as a cross-cultural interfaith dialogue where people of different cultural origins are sharing their beliefs through the placing of their differing traditions side by side without entering into debate about the veracity of the material being shared. However, it is not quite that simple because the participants in this conversation all bring some degree of prior knowledge with them into the dialogue. Robinson will bring his particular brand of missionary and cultural Christianity with him and also his sense of British superiority. Woorrady and the other mission Aboriginies will bring traditional knowledge and respect for that way of knowing. It is also the case that Woorrady and Robinson had known each other since the establishment of the Bruny Island Mission and had been fellow travellers over much of the previous couple of years.

It is now time to read the texts.

I proposed a question to my sable friends—how and where the first black man came from—to which question Woorrady gave in very full detail the traditional account of this and other subjects, as believed by all the natives along the southern and western coasts of the islands, and the natives assured me that the same tradition was believed by the whole of the natives in the island. The animated manner in which Woorrady related the several incidents gave considerable effect to the story, and the profound silence and attention of the rest and the assent to the veracity of his statements by two of the natives belonging to the south coast, rendered it still more interesting.

He stated that (moihernee?) made the black man first, that on his first formation he had a tail like a kangaroo and no joints in his knee;(droe.mer.deen.ne) he could never lay down and always had to stand up, and was obliged to sleep standing; that droe.mer.deen.ne cut off his tail and rubbed grease on the wound and made joints to his knees. He then for the first time sat on the ground and expressed his approbation of the comfort.

He said laller made all the rivers; he cut little streams and thus made big rivers. Said that he made the kangaroo out of the ground and that they run away; he described it by putting his hand on the ground and shewing how they came out and run away.

Said that two black men was asleep when a droegerdy came at night and scraped fire on them, that they called out 'be quiet', that he came again and again, and that at last they awaking caught hold of his leg, and after examining him and being much pleased they put him in the ground; and that afterwards they used to catch him and eat him. This was the first intimation of the badger (wombat).

Said that moihernee, who dwelt off Louisa Bay (Coxes Bight), used to fight with the devils; that plenty of devils dwelt at toogee low.

Woorrady said that moihernee made natives, that devils stopped in the ground and that moihernee took him out of the ground and made parlevar (Aboriginal person); that when he was first made he had a tail and no joint in his legs, that he could not sit down and always stood erect, that saw him in this situation and came to him and cut off his tail, rubbed grease over the wound and cured it and made joints to his knees and told the parlevar to sit down on the ground, that parlevar sat down and said it was nyerrae good, very good.

Said moihernee made all the rivers, that he cut the ground and made the rivers.

Droemerdeener is the bright star seen in the south. Woorrady says he comes out of the sea, because seen from Brune which is on the south part of the island he must necessarily do so.

Said that droemerdeene made kangaroo rat, that some natives were asleep when this animal made its appearance and that the rat came and threw stones at the natives, that the natives partly awoke and again slept, when he came again and threw more stones and repeated these visits till at length the native caught him and put him in the ground, that by and by he came out and stopped in the bush and that afterwards the natives eat him.

Woorrady says there is a large tree at Recherche Bay in which is cut the head of a man in large size and also children, that the natives call it wraeggowraper and that the children cry when they see it, that the native men destroyed it, and that this was done by the first white men.

Woorrady said that moinee and dromemerdeenne fight in the heavens and that moinee tumbled down at Louisa Bay and dwelt on the land, that his wife came after him and dwelt in the sea, and that by and by the moinee children came down in the rain and went into the wife's womb and that afterwards they had plenty of children.

Said that moinee fight the wraerggowraper. There is a great similarity this and Milton, where lucifer is hurled down from heaven.

Said that moinee cut the ground and made the rivers, cut the land and made the islands.

Said that wraerggowrapper is like a black man only very big and ugly, and that he travels like the wind, that he comes and watches the natives all night and before daylight comes he goes away like swift wind.

Said that the Tarner, that is boomer kangaroo, made the lymeenne, that is lagoons; that he sit down and make it.[1]

In conversation with Woorrady said that he saw the first ships come to VDL when they settled at Hobart Town, called Niberlooner; that the Py.dare natives speared some white men who landed in a boat, one man in the thigh; that white men went after the natives, the natives see them come but did not run away, saw their guns and said white men carry wood; that by and by white men shoot two blacks dead, when they all become frightened and run away. Said he saw the French discovery ships and that the men had white collars on. Said that the white man when they first came cut the head of a man on a tree and children, but the natives never destroyed it and that it is still there at Recherche Bay. Natives call it Wraerggowrapper, and when the children saw it they were frightened and run away. Said when they saw the first ship coming at sea they were frightened, and said it was Wraerggowrapper; that when the first people settled they cut down the trees, build houses, dug the ground and planted; that by and by more ships came, then at last plenty of ships; that the natives went to the mountains, and went and looked at what the white people did, went and told other natives and they came and looked also.[2]

Tonight; explained to the natives the Creation—of God, of the Flood &c—which I had frequently done when an opportunity afforded. They were very attentive. In conversation with them on the same subject:

Woorrady said that when the natives first saw the porcupine (echidna) that two of the natives was asleep and that the porcupine came and threw stones at them and hit them on the head, the forehead.

---

1. Plomley, *Friendly Mission*, 405–406.
2. Plomley, *Friendly Mission*, 408.

Said that laller the small piss ant perforated the penis.

Trugernanna said that the black women learn the girls to make baskets, to swim &c, and that the father puts a spear in the boy's hand and learns him to spear and to hunt.

They say that moinee was hurled from heaven and dwelt on the earth, and died and was turned to stone, and is at Coxes Bight, which was his own country. The natives say that there is a large stone standing up which is moinee and that he was a native and turned into this stone.[3]

Reflecting on this series of conversations

In these conversations about creation there is a lot going on. It is Robinson who initiates both conversations, The first one on the 7th of July and the second, a few days later, on the 12th of July. Robinson does this in the first instance by proposing a question to his Aboriginal companions about the creation of Aboriginal people. He initiates the second conversation by telling them stories from the first 11 chapters of Genesis. I would think it unlikely that Robinson read out these 11 chapters from his Bible. It would have been much more likely that he would have paraphrased the various stories together into one continuous narrative; leaving out the genealogies that connect them together. Robinson probably spoke in a way that interpreted these stories as history as would have been typical at the time. What we know as historical critical exegesis was only in its infancy in the early nineteenth century. He also indicates that his Aboriginal audience already had some familiarity with much of this material. From his comment it sounds like they were much more attentive on this occasion than previously. Perhaps asking questions in their turn.

By asking an open question about the way Aboriginal people were made, and by presenting he Biblical story in narrative terms without insisting on it being a universally authoritative account of 'the truth', Robinson is showing a willingness to listen to their stories. Woorrady responds by telling the story of the creation of people from his tradition. This then leads to opening up a wealth of creation stories from Aboriginal tradition. So, what we have here in this conversation

---

3. Plomley, *Friendly Mission*, 409.

is a yarning session around the campfire something that is very familiar in Aboriginal culture.

There are quite a lot of stories mentioned in these conversations. Some very brief where Robinson's notes only provide a name for a creation being and the particular animal created. Even these small snippets can still be seen to reflect the overall understanding of creation, and therefore of country/land. Giving all parts of country/land their own creation story shows the value given to each feature of the landscape, plant or animal which together a holistic vision of country/land. Other stories are more complex and reveal more about the complexity of the world view of pre-colonial Tasmania. Still others reflect the massive change brought by the colonisers. It will be these more complex stories and those that reflect the change brought by colonisation that are our main concern here. These particular stories concern the brothers Moihernee and Dromerdeenne, and also Wraerggowrapper.

We will start with Wraerggowrapper. We are given this description,

> Said that wraerggowrapper is like a black man only very big and ugly, and that he travels like the wind, that he comes and watches the natives all night and before daylight comes he goes away like swift wind.[4]

This does not sound like a character that anyone would want to meet. I would suggest that Wraerggowrapper represents the capacity within creation for things to go badly wrong, the experience of calamity or catastrophe. The comment that he 'watches the natives all night' leads to an apparently Tasmania wide ban on activities beyond the shelter of the campfires and the light and warmth that they provide. Nicholas Clements, in his book, The Black War, comments,

> The strength of this aversion is further evidenced by their unwillingness to launch night attacks, despite the tactical advantages this might have gained them.[5]

---

4. Plomley, *Friendly Mission*, 406.
5. Nicholas Clements, *The Black War* (St Lucia: University of Queensland Press, 2014), 111.

Movement at night has a range of perfectly natural risks. It's much easier to get lost. There is a much higher chance a falling and risking injury. In Tasmanian conditions there is also a risk of hypothermia. There is a sense in which banning night-time travel and other similar activities can be seen as what we might term sensible risk management. Keeping people in the safety of the light and warmth off the campfires, in a sheltered place, and away from a possible encounter with wraerggwrapper Is plain common sense.

Said that moinee fight the wraerggowrapper.[6]

This brief statement lets us know that there is tension between creation beings. This tension is also reflective of observed creation in country/land. Moihernee seeks to limit the influence in creation that can result in calamity and catastrophe. Moihernee seems to be concerned with sustainability and stability but must, fight for it. However, he also seems to be at odds with his brother, Dromerdeene.

The brothers we are told came across the stars. They fight about something (it is not clear what) and as a result Moihernee falls into the earth near Louisa Bay and dwelt in the land. His wife came after him and they had many children. Which accounts for the 'many devils' or creation beings that inhabit the land.

This brings us to the answer to the initial question that Robinson has asked to initiate this whole conversation about creation, 'how and where the first black man came from'. It is worth noting here that Robinson seems to have taken much more careful note of what he was told on this occasion than usual. He first records the story about the creation of the first black man by way of a paraphrase in the language he is most accustomed to. However, Robinson then seems to go back and check the story with Woorrady. He then re-records the story in language that is much more typical of Woorrady, In simpler more everyday English. It is the 2nd version that we will pay attention to.

> Woorrady said that moihernee made natives, that devils stopped in the ground and that moihernee took him out of the ground and made parlevar (Aboriginal person); that when he was first made he had a tail and no joint in his legs, that he could not sit down and always stood erect, that droemedeem saw him in this situation and came to him and cut off his tail, rubbed grease over the wound and cured it and made joints to

---

6. Plomley, *Friendly Mission*, 406.

his knees and told the parlevar to sit down on the ground, that parlevar sat down and said it was nyerrae good, very good.[7]

Moihernee is the main actor in this story. First, he takes a devil (which we have so far thought of as Moihernee's children or further creation beings) out of the ground with which to make this Aboriginal people. This idea that creation beings can be thought of a first or original ancestors of the creatures they create it's not all that unusual in Aboriginal stories. However, this information is not as significant for our purpose then the actual shape that Moihernee gives to this first black man. He is given the form of a type of kangaroo. From the waist up this first person what we would normally know as a modern human but from there down has the body of a kangaroo. This remarkable creature is consistent with the rest of Australian creation where nearly all mammals are marsupials, the only exceptions being sea mammals, and the monotremes, echidna and platypus.

At this point in the story Droemedeeme intervenes. It gets rid of the kangaroo parts leaving a modern human who can sit comfortably on the ground. And Woorrady tells us this was 'nyerrae good, very good'.[8]

Instead of being left the way Moihernee made him this Aboriginal person is no longer a consistent part of creation with all the other animals. This change has left him/her distinct from the rest of creation. The initial explanation given about being able to sit comfortably on the ground appears to be a bit superficial. Kangaroos don't seem to be at all uncomfortable lounging in the shade on sunny afternoons. So, the question of why we are not kangaroos continues to linger. When the first people arrived on the Australian continent some sixty or seventy thousand years ago, they would have found themselves in an alien world where most of the fauna and flora were nothing like anything they would have seen before. Climatic conditions would also have challenged them. Working out how to simply survive would have been a huge challenge. The feeling of being aliens in a strange land would have been strong.

As this story comes from the southernmost region of the continent, the last place to be reached by first people, I wonder if the story might reflect this very early question of survival. Could it have been carried

---

7. Plomley, *Friendly Mission*, 406.
8. Plomley, *Friendly Mission*, 406.

by the leading edge of the slowly advancing wave of settlement in this strange country/land? Could it be a part of the very early learning story about learning to live on country/land? Is this story about this new human creature having to find a way to connect with country/land and all its other residents?

These questions will lead to a process of lifelong learning about the right way to live on country/land. In doing this kinship relationships and totemic relationships will be discovered, and along with those relationships, responsibilities of custodianship and management of country/land. A journey of knowledge will have begun.

So far, we have talked about simple creation stories with one creation/original ancestor being Involved with a single act of creation. We have also talked about the stories with tension between creation/ancestor beings. In both of these cases we have been considering the material in this conversation between Robinson and his Aboriginal companions, With Woorrady being the main source of the information. We have also noted that his Aboriginal friends have been firm supporters of the veracity of Woorrady's stories. All of this has been done in a way that is reflective of the precolonial context of Aboriginal life in southern Tasmania. It is now appropriate to look at two stories from those conversations that show a colonial era re-thinking about the roles of the key players in this collection of creation stories.

The first concerns developments in the Wraerggowrapper material. The Second will concern Moihernee and Droemerdenne.

> In conversation with Woorrady said that he saw the first ships come to VDL when they settled at Hobart Town, called Niberlooner; that the Py.dare natives speared some white men who landed in a boat, one man in the thigh; that white men went after the natives, the natives see them come but did not run away, saw their guns and said white men carry wood; that by and by white men shoot two blacks dead, when they all become frightened and run away. Said he saw the French discovery ships and that the men had white collars on. Said that the white man when they first came cut the head of a man on a tree and children, but the natives never destroyed it and that it is still there at Recherche Bay. Natives call it Wraerggowrapper, and when the children saw it they were frightened and run away. Said when they saw the first

ship coming at sea they were frightened, and said it was Wraerggowrapper; that when the first people settled they cut down the trees, build houses, dug the ground and planted; that by and by more ships came, then at last plenty of ships; that the natives went to the mountains, and went and looked at what the white people did, went and told other natives and they came and looked also.[9]

I quote this passage in full because it not only gives an account of the European invasion from an Aboriginal perspective but also illustrates how this invasion was interpreted by Aboriginal people. In the space of a couple of years Aboriginal people had witnessed the 1802 semi-permanent camp of the French expedition at Recherche Bay. The following year Lt Bowen had arrived in the Derwent estuary and some months later Col. Collins had established his base at Sullivan's Cove and permanent British settlement had begun.

> *they cut down the trees, build houses, dug the ground and planted; that by and by more ships came.*[10]

This is the beginning of profound change that that will not turn out well for Aboriginal people. This change is accompanied by violence. Aboriginal people soon learn what muskets can do. The strangers seem to know nothing of proper protocols nor to show any desire to learn. The also seemed to have no proper concern for country/land. They just turn up and do what they want, where they want, with no thought about asking. There is also no respect for Aboriginal law or culture. It is as though these newcomers are blind to the very existence of the proper way of doing things, that has (to the Aboriginal mind) always existed.

Quite early on it seems this invasion was interpreted in terms of an increase in the strength and influence of Wraerggowrapper. If we follow Woorrady's story the carving of a head on a tree, probably having no more significance to the French than the graffiti of a bored sailor, is where this tradition of the rising power of Wraerggowrapper begins panning out as a way to understand the true meaning of the European invasion.

---

9. Plomley, *Friendly Mission*, 408.
10. Plomley, *Friendly Mission*, 408.

We may ask where Droemerdenne and Moihernee fit into this changed scenario. Other than his pivotal role in the creation of the first people, Droemerdenne is also given credit for creating the kangaroo rat. Beyond these acts of creation, Droemerdenne is associated with the stars. He fights with Moihernee causing the fall to Louisa Bay and all that follows from that. '*Droemerdeener is the bright star seen in the south*' we are told. It seems that he does not dwell in the land in the same way as all the other creation beings. We are also told,

> Woorrady says he comes out of the sea, because seen from Brune which is on the south of the island he must necessarily do so.[11]

This is suggestive of Droemerdenne is not being of the land but of sea country. This would imply that his relationships are with sea creatures rather than land creatures. Is he related to the seal and the whale and so on? Which interestingly are also placental mammals like people of the kind that he modifies. The southeast and south people such as Woorrady and his companion as both land and sea people given their expertise with watercraft and visits to large and small offshore islands and seal hunting. Is there a connection here? I'm not really sure on such small evidence, but I would not be surprised to discover that something like this could be the case. Not being a resident of country/land on land, he is not a creation being whose principal activity is discernible easily from the relation to country/land. So, what is happening, the British invasion, is perhaps of concern for Droemerdenne, in relation to whaling and sealing operations.

On one earlier occasion some years ago when I first tried to do some analysis on these stories, I attempted to work with western concepts of transcendence and immanence without much success. At that time, I thought of Droemerdenne as being, in some sense, transcendent because of his continuing association with the stars. He does not fall to the land like his brother. This idea may still have something to offer. Droemerdenne, it seems, can operate as a creator in both land and sea country without falling from his star. He changes the form of the first people from marsupial to placental mammals in opposition to Moihernee, without pushback. He also does his own little bit with the creation of the kangaroo rat. There

---

11. Plomley, *Friendly Mission*, 406.

are hints of a freedom of operation here that is beyond that of the other creation beings. In the material we have he is not one who fights Wraerggowrapper or other creation beings in the ground.

However, this is certainly not the case for Moihernee. We are told he fights with "devils in the ground." And specifically, he fights with Wraerggowrapper to bring stability and sustainability to country/land and the people. In the context of this Wraerggowrapper take over we might well ask what has happened to Moihernee, where is he and why is he not doing his job?

At the end of the entries in Robinson's journal for these creation conversations offers us this story,

> They say that moinee was hurled from heaven and dwelt on the earth, and died and was turned to stone, and is at Coxes Bight, which was his own country. The natives say that there is a large stone standing up which is moinee and that he was a native and turned into this stone.[12]

This story gives us important pieces of information about Moihernee that we haven't heard before. We are told that he died, was turned into stone, and that he is at Coxes Bight which is his own country/land. This story certainly gives us an understanding of why Moihernee is no longer able to resist, or hold back, the activity of Wraerggowrapper. Moihernee is now as inactive as a big lump of rock.

When we see the word 'died', our first assumption might be something like, gone forever, consigned to history, and not coming back. A bit more reflection might be appropriate here. Moihernee is a creation being and has effectively been buried on his 'own country'. There is the well-known Aboriginal tradition about the importance of Aboriginal people/ancestors needing to be laid to rest on their own country/land. This is important spiritually for both the spirit of the deceased person and for the health of country/land. The connection to country/land must be maintained even in death. Moihernee may become active again at some point. The signs of this would be any evidence detected in country/land of a return to stability and sustainability following the present Wraerggowrapper chaos.

At the time of these conversations both the colonial government and Robinson's mission aborigines were overestimating Aboriginal

---

12. Plomley, *Friendly Mission*, 409.

numbers. On the earlier expedition along the south and west coast had encountered several apparently healthy communities and even on this trip has recently seen signs of recent Aboriginal activity. Around this time the Aboriginal population of the settled areas (the eastern half of Tasmania) was thought to be still about 500, when in fact it was probably only 100.[13] Add the 500 to those seen on the west coast and the total starts to look somewhere in the region of 1000. If a safe haven could be established, with these types of numbers, the hope of some reasonable degree of stability could be imagined by this group of Aboriginal people.

It is important to remember that the dramatic change in circumstances that resulted from the colonial invasion was not the first time Aboriginal Tasmania had suffered catastrophic change. The ending of the ice age at the start of the Holocene cut off communication with their mainland cousins. This may have happened quite suddenly.

In her book Lyndall Ryan includes some maps of sea level rise and fall during the Palaeolithic era.[14] She also includes a chart of the actual changes in sea level by comparison to present depths. Looking at these maps and sea level tables enable us to see that between 40,000 and 14,000 before the present, the eastern land route between Wilson's Promontory and northeast Tasmania, via the Furneaux Islands, was open. In the period around 18,000 before the present the western route, via King Island, would also have been open. That these two routes were open and were both taken advantage of is supported by linguistic analysis done by A.J. Taylor. His analysis of place names indicates linguistic connection with Victoria for the eastern route, and connections with parts of southeast South Australia and adjacent parts of southwest Victoria.[15] Archaeological evidence also supports the presence of Aboriginal people in Tasmania from at least 40,000 years ago. This also means that during this long period of Aboriginal settlement in Tasmania reasonably frequent communication and connection to the mainland for trade and the movement of new knowledge could have continued.

The sea level table indicates that in 18,000 years before the present the sea level would have been about 115 metres lower than present

---

13. Clements, *The Black War*, 158.
14. Ryan, *Tasmanian Aborigines*, 4–5.
15. AJ Taylor, Unpublished draft, Not completed before his death.

and an increase of roughly 30 metres would have been sufficient to close the western route. A further 30 or so metres would have been enough to close the eastern route, still being about 55 metres below present. Between these two routes the middle part of Bass Strait would have been a vast saltmarsh for most of the time and perhaps, around 18,000 years before the present a large shallow lake fed by both Victorian rivers and Tasmania's main northern rivers, making a central route problematic.

The creation of vast and deep continental ice sheets takes a very long time. They need a lot of moisture. This comes in the form of rain and snow, mostly snow. A few hundred millimetres each year. However, their melting can be a far more rapid and chaotic process. As temperature begins to exceed zero degrees Celsius, several different things begin to happen to accelerate the change from ice to liquid water. At first the ice resists melting because of its ability to reflect sunlight. Slightly more warming defeats this creating liquid ice lakes in all the hollows and dips on the surface caused by variations in the underlying ground. In steeper areas gravity starts to play an increasing role as the ice slides downhill. Ice dams form in narrow valleys then collapse under the pressure of liquid water building up. On coastline rising seawater undermines the ice sheets causing further collapse. In the end there will be catastrophic floods, sometimes of enormous size. All of this is going to be noticed by coastal people all around the world. Perhaps within a generation of two what was a large peninsular becomes an island when a storm cuts the last narrow connection.

Slowly everything restabilises. Moihernee emerges and Wraerggowrapper is restrained, and the surviving people adapt to a new set of circumstances.

The challenge that faces Woorrady and his people is not a massive natural event. It is an invasion by a civilisation with massively different technologies and ways of understanding the world and their place in it. This is Wraerggowrapper set loose by people with little concern for the consequences.

Chapter 7
Return to 1838 and the Sermon

Accommodation or Critique?

At the end of the section where we examined Woorrady's sermon we arrived at a question asking about whether, or not, we should regard it in terms of accommodation or critique of the prevailing mission theology. I suspect that there is much more critique than accommodation. There are several insights that we should consider from the above discussion of the stories that were shared on the theme of creation, both Aboriginal and biblical, in northeast Tasmania seven years earlier.

When we looked at the complex of stories It seems that there was a story for every aspect of creation. The creation of each creature, or part of the landscape, we saw a creation being involved in the process. In some cases, this creation being may have been involved in other acts of creation. It is highly likely that there are many stories of the same kind belonging to pre-colonial Aboriginal culture. It is as though for any question that a child, adult or stranger may ask, there will be a story within the whole complex of stories about creation and country/land that will answer the question. It is evident that there is no particular valuing of one part of creation or country/land over another. Everything has its unique place and role and is to be valued accordingly. There was nothing in these stories to indicate any sort of creation being, or human, hierarchy. So, the operative theology of creation could well be described as non-hierarchical but giving value to all no matter how large or small.

This pattern of talking about creation and country/land also indicates that the theology of creation is about present reality as much as it is about beginnings. The linear sense of time that is so much a part of western/mainstream thinking is absent here. Some of these stories such as the one about the creation of the first people may be incredibly ancient. The issue of why people are not kangaroos could go right back to the beginnings of human occupation of Australia. But at the same time, we have also seen that these stories can be updated to fit the contemporary context should there be great change.

The Wraerggowrapper material is a clear example of this. The identification of the Europeans as a manifestation of Wraerggowrapper seems to have begun (according to Woorrady) with the extended visit of the French in 1802, before the first British settlement and has its origins in the behaviour of these Frenchmen. They, knowing it or not, were persistently operating outside of Aboriginal law. The Wraerggowrapper material is appropriately extended to include them. It is updated for the new reality that the people face.

It is worth noting here that in this collection of creation stories that we have been examining there is no creation act that is associated with Wraerggowrapper. We have been seeing him as one of the creation beings; is this in a sense a bit odd? Wraerggowrapper has been characterised as the capacity for things to go badly wrong, or that aspect of creation representing calamity or catastrophe. If we consider such events, (while we would not want to be caught up in one, or more of them) they can sometimes be things that create space for something new to happen. The forest tree that falls during a storm creates a sunny space for new plants to grow.

The second example of changing stories concerns Moihernee in his role as the one who fights Wraerggowrapper. What is fascinating here is that this seems to be an adaptation of the older story of Moihernee's fall from the stars. This makes it abundantly clear that we are talking about the same creation being. This time he lands on his own country/land a bit further west where there is a large rock, as an in-country/land marker for this story. This story goes on to tell us that he is dead and turned to stone, thus giving an explanation for the ever-increasing expansion of the Wraerggowrapper/British, lawlessness and potential for things to go badly wrong.

These two stories alone are enough for us to see that there is an openness to change and adaptation. Incorporating changes into the holistic Aboriginal story patterns was indeed possible. Development of new understandings in regard to the intertwined relationship between spirituality and observation of country/land certainly seems to be happening here. While we can see all of this from the changing stories this alone does not immediately indicate what should be done about it.

The event that had taken place during the time of rapid increase of sea level rise some 10,000 years or so before the present could be comparable in scale to the British invasion. However, the same solution would not be appropriate. Back then the response was perhaps less urgent. While some land was lost to the sea the high country/land would have become more accessible. Developing improved watercraft also would have maintained accessibility to hills and mountains that had become close offshore islands and peninsulas. Changes in vegetation types as the climate both warmer and wetter could also be managed. Some rearrangement of clan territory would have been needed in some contexts as well.

This new Wraerggowrapper event that Woorrady experienced over his lifetime was an invasion by another people who were treating country/land in very different ways. Earlier we noted that at the time of the conversations in 1831 there was still an expectation that the Aboriginal population was still of a viable size. By 1838, and Woorrady's sermon, we know that this was not the case, as did he. Both the colonial side and the Aboriginal side had vastly overestimated the size of the Aboriginal population and its unhealthy demographic. Disproportionate numbers of men and women and so few children. The full extent of the disaster had become apparent. Just this few gathered at Wybelena were almost all that were left. The Mission was it.

There is another theological theme present in this recognition of the calamity that has overtaken Woorrady and his people. This is the theme of Theodicy. This takes two forms. First, the destruction of people, culture, and the exile of the few survivors. This has similarities to other genocidal crimes against humanity that we may be aware of, taking the form of the question; why do bad things happen to innocent/good people, if God is good?

The second form concerns country/land. We have noted earlier the close connection between country/land, the stories and the people. It is country/land that is also being changed by the invasion. In his own time Woorrady will have noticed this change and will have seen it as inappropriate treatment of country/land. Whalers and sealers have decimated local populations of these animals. On land, in some places kangaroos have almost been wiped out and the emu is on the way to extinction in Tasmania. These animals are being replaced by European livestock. Various pests have arrived with the invaders, rats and mice. Also, various weed seeds (such as gorse) have arrived with the sheep. There has been extensive timber cutting and stone quarrying. The ways in which this is being managed is clearly more about exploitation than in the tradition of good long term custodial management familiar to Aboriginal people. The health of country/land is itself under threat from the settlers. We might term this as ecological theodicy.

When we raise this issue of theodicy it is recognised in the traditional stories through the Wraerggowrapper material. However, the British invasion is so serious that its designation as a Wraerggowrapper event raises the theodicy question to a much higher level. It can no longer be contained by Moihernee or by Aboriginal bans on certain activities. By identifying the way forward for the younger generation as the creator God of the missionaries Woorrady is passing the theodicy question onto the Christian creator God.

Having spoken of the significance of the British invasion, Woorrady then offers,

> we ought to be fond of one another. We ought to love God. God made everything, the salt water, the horse, the bullock, the opossum, the wallaby, the kangaroo and wombat. Love him and you go to him bye and bye.[1]

What we are interested in at this point is the notion of God as creator for everyone listening. Both the assembled Aboriginal people and the British officers and staff.

If we recall that on the 12th of July seven years earlier Robinson notes when telling the Genesis stories that he had, 'frequently done when an opportunity afforded'.[2]

There is by this time little doubt that Woorrady both knew and understood these Genesis 1–11 stories. He has certainly got the point that the God that the missionaries were so keen on is to be understood as the creator of everything. Also, it would be difficult to believe that this master of traditional Aboriginal story telling had not

---

1. Plomley, *Weep in Silence*, 733.
2. Plomley, *Friendly Mission*, 409.

got the obvious point of these stories. Everything starts off good with this Biblical version of creation. However, it keeps going wrong. The first people break the only taboo that they are given and so are cast out of the garden and now must work for a living. Then their son's fallout and the farmer kills the shepherd, and is further exiled. Then when there are many people, this law breaking, Wraerggowrapper type, behaviour gets so bad that this creator God tries pushing the reset button with the one good family he can find. The great flood happens but this whole process fails to work. Instead, everyone gets together and attempts to build a tower to heaven, essentially an assault on the Creator. Splitting them up into different peoples with different languages might gain some breathing space but it is not a solution.

Woorrady can probably see that these stories, although recognisably creation stories, also reflect the present reality of the British just as do the stories of his people. Right from the start they are about people becoming, farmers and shepherds and builders of towns and cities, clearing and alienating country/land rather than learning from it. The unhealthy relationship of the British to country/land is already apparent in their creation stories. The evidence of his own eyes tells him that the behaviour of the British matches the problems that the Creator God is facing. These issues are right there in the Genesis stories. They are willing to use violence to get what they want. They ignore the need to work with the rest of creation in custodial ways. The British seek power and control over people and country/land and are apparently uninterested in the sustainability and stability, the work of Moihernee. They seem happy to take the risk of letting Wraerggowrapper loose. They simply do not see the danger, perhaps even wanting to utilise Wraerggowrapper power to enhance their accumulation of control.

Woorrady also seems to realise that he and his people are being treated by British as little children rather than as responsible adults. On the one hand they are being encouraged to adopt a new story about one Creator God who ought to be in a relationship to all people based on love, while at the same time trying to frighten people into heaven with the threat of hell. Woorrady is bright enough to notice some inconsistency in this. It seems to be more about power and control than grace and love.

When it comes to this situation of sermons/testimonies that all the senior Aboriginal men are being asked to be part of, Woorrady needs to be careful. He must do his best to find hope for the younger people in his audience but also not provoke the officers and staff of the mission into believing that he is inciting rebellion. So Woorrady begins with a simple but clear statement of basic facts that have led to the current situation of his people but avoids assigning blame. Even the people in charge of the mission cannot deny the short statements regarding the facts of recent history. He then says, 'We ought to love God' and characterises God as creator of everything including the 'horse and the bullock', the most powerful of the new animals brought by the British. Woorrady then recommends loving this creator God so as to go to this God, 'bye and bye'. Woorrady then simply avoids saying anything at all about hell and damnation. He avoids playing the British game about salvation as being somehow about being a good subject of the empire.

Conclusions and possible ways forward

Having worked our way through this second part it is time to propose some provisional conclusions. Having introduced the topic in general terms in the Introduction. It spoke about the experiment of living on country in a twenty-first century way and also gave some insight into my personal journey into Aboriginal identity and ways of knowing. Chapter four was about appropriate language, Hermeneutical and epistemological issues. It also included some detailed discussion about creation/original ancestor beings in the context of Aboriginal spirituality. Chapter five gave us an introduction to Woorrady's remarkable 1838 sermon and its context. Chapter six worked through the complex of stories that were a part of the 1831 conversations with Robinson on the theme of creation to help us further understand the theology of Woorrady. Chapter seven has seen a return to the 1838 sermon and has allowed further reflection on its significance.

From the discussion of Woorrady's theology there are some key points that we can take forward with us.

Firstly, the capacity of the stories to change as the situation with country/land changes. This capacity indicate that we need to see Woorrady's theology as an open system. A theological system that is open to and relevant to the world of today, which is very different to the world he experienced some two centuries ago. In this context a question of the nature of Woorrady's theology arises about the relationship of God and creation. Is this theology a form or pantheism or panentheism? If we ignore the stories about Dromerdeene and just focus on the resident creation beings in country/land then, the closeness of relationship between the stories and the current context of country/land may well indicate a form of pantheism. However, inclusion of The Droemerdenne material suggests a form of panentheism. He does not dwell in country/land but remains in the stars. Given that it is assumed that the Aboriginal world view of the first Tasmanians is in some sense pre-Copernican the stars are thought of as heaven. It is not only his location that is important here. Dromerdeene seems to have a freedom to intervene in creation in ways beyond the capacity of the other creation beings. These features hint at a panentheism in Woorrady's theology because they indicate an element of transcendence on the part of Droemerdenne.

Second, we can also affirm that the typology of struggle between the stability and sustainability of Moihernee and the capacity to go badly wrong represented by Wraerggowrapper is still valid as a way of understanding a wide range of issues in the present day. This is particularly relevant to climate change, loss of biodiversity, plastic pollution, acidification of the oceans and depleted availability of fresh water. I would also include here those human behaviours and systems that are major contributors to this situation.

Third, in his 1838 sermon Woorrady points us towards the Christian doctrine of creation and salvation without any sign of having become a Christian. He uses the word God, which he knows will mean the Christian God both to his aboriginal audience and the British colonisers, when he speaks of creation. He ends this sermon by saying, 'Love him and you go to him'. I suspect that here we see him interpreting what he knows about Christian beliefs on the afterlife as something similar to his traditional beliefs where the spirits of the dead return to country/land after death. This could also be in tune with love of a Christian creator God as the means of salvation.

These three points may be somewhat speculative on limited evidence, but they are suggestive of the need for further theological work.

**Part 3 The God-Creation Story
(Christian Perspective)**

Chapter 8
Introduction

In this third part It is intended to explore some of the themes from the second part through a contemporary Christian perspective. It is not intended to give commentary on all parts of Christian theology. Instead, we will follow some of the themes that have emerged from the previous section. In particular the Wraerggowrapper designation.

We will begin with brief survey of global history over the past couple of centuries since Woorrady's time in order to bring ourselves up to date. This will include something of my own journey.

We will then move onto Wraerggowrapper designation dynamic from two perspectives. Firstly, looking at the problem of evil from a philosophical and scientific perspective. Secondly looking at Biblical and theological perspectives on the same issues. In mainstream culture this issue is usually called 'the problem of evil'. Here I am choosing to use Wraerggowrapper designation to describe this issue for the following reasons. Initially because as a Tasmanian aboriginal person I want to be consistent with Woorrady's designation of the issue. I am also aware that the traditional mainstream thought tends to distinguish between human evil and natural evil. This distinction is problematic from an Aboriginal point of view. Aboriginal worldviews tend to be holistic. We can recall from the discussion in part two that Wraerggowrapper events can be natural and/or human based. Another issue here concerns the use of the word 'evil'. In some contexts, evil is understood to have connotations of deliberate malice or the deliberate breaching of moral or ethical norms. The type of events included in the discussion of this topic may include unintended consequences of actions that seemed ok at the time, and others that seem to have little to do with any kind of conscious decision making at all.

Some may wonder why I want to look at this issue from the perspective of science as well as theology. Over the past couple of centuries there have been many advances in scientific fields that have broadened our understanding of the nature of ways we may view evil. One consequence of these advances in scientific knowledge is the human ability to mitigate evil, or the Wraerggowrapper effect, have grown enormously. Advances in engineering have enabled better flood control and building technology that mitigates the damage earthquakes. The growth in microbiology has mitigated the devastating effects of many once common illnesses. This mitigating ability can be described in Woorrady's terms as Moihernee fighting Wraerggowrapper. On top of all this one of the fundamental assumptions operating in this book is that no matter which discipline we are working with, we are always dealing with one world: with a holistic understanding of creation.

Bringing the Story up to Date

From the period of the enlightenment, beginning in the early seventeenth century, began a growing sense in European society of upward progress. This sense of progress would become the dominant theme providing positive meaning to European civilization. In the twentieth century this theme of continuous upward progress began to hit some serious roadblocks. This has raised questions of Theodicy, the justification of God's goodness in the face of the fact of evil.[1] In this chapter we will first rehearse the main geo-political events that have made this issue so prominent. Second, we will explore the philosophical and theological problems that surround the fact of evil.

In chapter 5 we looked at the general historical and philosophical picture in mainstream European society to understand the theology of mission that Woorrady encountered. It is important now to bring ourselves up to date. A lot has changed in the past couple of centuries. We have seen some of the trends that we looked at earlier accelerate dramatically. The development of science and a consequent change in the way we understand the universe has expanded on many fronts. Huge movement has consequently emerged in technology and the

---

1. John Hick, 'The problem of Evil', in *Philosophy and Contemporary Issues*, edited by John R Burr and Milton Goldinger, second edition (New York: Macmillan, 1976).127.

expansion of both manufacturing and communications industry. The theological landscape has also experienced dramatic change with the advent of various forms for philosophical atheism. Politically Karl Marx has described religion as, 'the opiate of the masses.' Freud has called it an 'illusion' and Nietzsche declared the 'death of God.' Massive social and political change has also occurred. In western style democracies we have seen a profound shift towards universal enfranchisement as opposed to only male voters from political and economic elites. During the twentieth century most of Asia eastern Europe and parts of central America and Africa have had autocratic governments based on Marxist philosophy rather than monarchy. Medical knowledge and capability, along with food production, and distribution has dramatically increased life expectancy.

This is largely, a somewhat positive view of change in the increasingly secular history of the world. During the second half the 19th century there was a dramatic increase in industrialization going well beyond its beginnings in England's industrial revolution. Industrialization was accelerating in all of Europe and North America and, also Japan. Most of the nation states, that were experiencing this growing industrialization, also had their eyes on consolidating and expanding their colonial interests. At the same time communications around the world increased dramatically. Steam technology allowed the development of railways and steamships. The movement of goods, people and information became much more reliable and quicker, and possible for much larger numbers. Later came telegraph communications and by the early 20th century radio communications. This enabled almost instant communications and consequently more efficient administration of global empires. From a European perspective this is being seen as an age of progress. From the perspective of those people who had been colonised these developments would not have been seen quite so positively.

The downside of this age of progress was soon to become apparent. Towards the end of the 19th century and at the beginning of the twentieth century a massive arms race was going on between the major European powers. Alliances were made. On the one side were central European powers, Germany and the Austro-Hungarian empire and the Ottoman empire. On the other side were Britain, France, and Imperial Russia. In 1914 War broke out. It was intended to be over in a few months, but instead, it developed into brutal trench warfare that would persist with little movement despite the enormous forces deployed on both sides, for four years. Battle front casualties on both sides numbered in their millions. By the end of the war the USA had also been drawn into the conflict. The Bolshevik revolution had occurred in Russia and the first Marxist state was being consolidated.

The eventual peace treaty was also not much better. Not only did Germany lose its few colonial possessions and small contested border territories but was also forced to change its form of government to a democratic republic and hit with huge financial reparations. The Austro-Hungarian empire was dismantled forming a number of smaller independent nations, The Ottoman Empire had lost most of its middle eastern possessions, large parts of which were taken over by the British and French. The Treaty of Versailles also placed severe restrictions on the German military, in an attempt to prevent any capacity to start a future European war. The treaty was seen as punishment and humiliation by many in Germany. The seeds of further conflict in Europe had been sown.

In the early 1920's Germany experienced hyperinflation and economic hardship while the rest of the industrialised world seemed to be enjoying a post war boom. During this time the radical right-wing politics of fascism was emerging in Italy. In Germany the national socialists party emerged, with Hitler as one of its leaders, and attempted a coup. It failed and the leaders were imprisoned. However, it was a political movement that picked up on the resentment that had followed on the treaty of Versailles and was willing to use latent antisemitic racism to scapegoat everything that had gone wrong for Germany. They had also shown that they were happy to use violence and intimidation as part of their political strategy.

We need to remember that during this period of history racism was often seen as a legitimate part of government policy in many countries, including democratic ones. Australia had its white Australia policy and its assimilation and mission reserves policies for aboriginal people. We must also note that antisemitism was often supported by Christian Churches and had been since the Middle Ages. Restrictions on where Jews could live and how they could participate in economic activity was unfairly limited by law in many parts of Europe.

1929 had seen the stock market crash and the beginning of the Great Depression. In difficult economic times it is easier for radical political groups to gain political traction. By 1933 Hitler's National Socialists had achieved electoral success and he had become chancellor. Anti-

Jewish legislation could be passed and began to come into increasing effect. Hitler by this point is rapidly consolidating his power not only over his own party but also the military and other social institutions, including the state church.

Internationally Hitler is starting to circumvent the limitations of Treaty of Versailles. Aero clubs to train pilots, youth and sporting organisations were promoted to ensure a ready supply of personal already trained in basic ways, so as to be able to rapidly build up the military. Alongside of this were also the paramilitary organisations within the Nazi party itself. The navy is also being upgraded with modern ships, frequently pushing the technical limits of the treaty. Germany's small air force and other military was also gaining experience in the Spanish civil war in support of the right-wing forces of General Franco. By 1938 Hitler had also, with a combination of force and clever diplomacy, gotten back virtually all the small border territories lost at the end of the first world war and had drawn Austria into the fold.

Fascism had already been seemingly working well in Italy under Mussolini. The vision of an empire centred on ancient Rome also seemed to be developing with the military campaign in Abyssinia. An alliance between the two fascist states was on. At the same time on the other side of the world Japan was strengthening its military and expanding its ambitions in Asia and the Pacific. Taking advantage of the instability and armed conflict in several provinces afflicting the central government, Japan had invaded northern China, seizing all of Manchuria by force. By the late 1930's the scene had been set for global conflict.

The second world war proved to be much worse than the first one had been. There were multiple theatres of war, both in Europe, Asia and the Pacific. The tactics of combining the newer technologies of aircraft and tanks with the movement of armies enabled attackers to break through entrenched defenders more easily. Bombing from much larger aircraft made attacks on industrial infrastructure and cities beyond the front much more destructive. Armies both advanced and retreated much more frequently and over much larger distances. Tens of millions of civilians became caught up in it. Civilian deaths outnumbered those of the battle fronts. Many more civilians became displaced and homeless, living in nightly terror of the bombing raids. Still more went hungry or were put into forced labour battalions to do dangerous work on minimal rations.

It was not until close to the end of this war that the full extent of various atrocities and the sheer scale of the damage became apparent. As the allied armies advanced into Poland and Germany the network of Nazi death camps was revealed and the industrialised murder of more than six million people, mostly Jews, became known. The German theologian Jurgen Moltmann describes the impact this revelation had on him, and others, as a teenage prisoner of war at the end of war in Europe,

> The break-up of the German front, the collapse of law and humanity, the self-destruction of German civilization and culture, and finally the appalling end on 9 May 1945—all this was followed by the revelation of the crimes which had been committed in Germany's name—Buchenwald, Auschwitz, Maidanek, Bergen-Belsen and the rest. And with that came the necessity of standing up to it all inwardly, shut up in camps as we were. I think my own little world fell to pieces then too . . . In that Belgian camp, hungry as we were, I saw how other men collapsed inwardly, how they gave up all hope, sickening for the lack of it, some of them dying. The same thing almost happened to me.[2]

The 'peace' at the end of war in Europe is perhaps better described as an armed ceasefire between rival superpowers. The Prime Minister of Britain, Churchill, The President of the USA, Roosevelt, and the leader of the Soviet Union, Stalin, met shortly before the end of the war to redraw the map of Europe. Germany was divided into four military administration areas between the Soviets, France, Britain and the USA. Berlin was divided into four. Later this arrangement became East and West Germany, and East and West Berlin. Stalin was left with effective control of most of eastern Europe.

The end of the war with Japan came a few months later. It followed the use by the USA of newly developed nuclear weapons. Two of Japan's cities were destroyed within a few days, creating close to 200,000 casualties in total by two aircraft dropping one bomb each. The message was clear, surrender unconditionally or face the total destruction of your country and people.

---

2. Jurgen Moltmann, *Experiences of God* (Philadelphia: Fortress Press, 1980), 7.

In the years following the Japanese surrender the two largest Asian countries achieved their independence. British India had done so relatively peacefully but the decision to partition the sub-continent into two separate nations based on Islamic majority or Hindu majority caused considerable ethnic tension, rioting and mass internal migrations of people fleeing the violence. In China the struggle against the Japanese had enhanced the support for the communist insurgency. Following the war, with Soviet support, it managed to force the government forces out of mainland China within four years. There were also attempts by some of the colonial powers to re-establish their control over former colonies.

By the 1950's patterns were emerging. The Soviet Union had gained a number of German scientists and with their help had developed both rocket and nuclear technology, including the bomb. The USA had also gained German rocket scientist and Britain and France had also developed nuclear weapons. Communist China was not far behind. The international strategic situation was now dominated by two superpowers, the USA and the Soviet Union. This situation was known as the "cold war." It is in this context, where direct conflict may well result in mutual destruction, that the process of decolonisation in particularity Asian and African contexts takes on the character of a dangerous proxy war between the superpowers. The Soviets, and Chinese, supporting communist insurgencies with military equipment and training while the USA and its allies gave similar support to just about any other regime (Military dictatorships, emergent democracies, corrupt presidents etc) that was not communist. This situation with some warming up and liberalisation at times continued to be the post-World War II reality up until the collapse of the Soviet Union in the late 1980's.

Unfortunately, the history of war, the violence of human against human does not end there. In the late 20th century, we heard of the killing fields of Cambodia with estimates of over two million dead. We also learned the phrase, 'ethnic cleansing', a euphonism for mass murder during the Bosnian war and saw the horror of the mass slaughter of Tutsis by their Hutu neighbours in Rwanda. Even today as I write this there is war in Ukraine, continuing conflict in the Middle East, parts of Africa and southern Asia. Just on this basis Woorrady's designation of mainstream civilisation as Wraerggowrapper still appears to be appropriate. The evil of human against human is still very much a problem plaguing the world. The question of how Christian theology responds to this situation is very relevant.

Almost up to Date

In picking up the story since the time of Woorrady, I want to pause for a moment in the late 20th century. I have chosen this period for two reasons. First, it was the time in which some ground-breaking books of Christian theology were published, in particular by Hans Kung and Jurgen Moltmann. Christian apologetics and Trinitarian theology were beginning to become significant live discussions for practically the first time since the fifth century. Second, it was the time when I began to re-engage with the Church as a young man.

Towards the end of 1975 my stepfather had accepted a new ministry placement with the Methodist Church in Rural Victoria. After seven years of stability in Hobart we were to be on the move. I was about to finish year twelve. I was 17 years old at the time and had a degree of financial independence as a Commonwealth Scholarship recipient. The plan was for me to study forest science at Melbourne University, assuming I passed my end of year exams. In the Tasmanian matriculation system at the time this meant passing at least four Level 3 subjects over the course of two years. This would give me university entrance. As it turned out I only managed to achieve three full passes and one lower pass, this was not quite enough for university entrance. I was greatly relieved because the prospect of moving to country Victoria away from my friends and spending most of the year in the big city and having to establish a whole set of new friendships in a vastly different context was scary indeed. In the end it was decided that I could stay in Hobart with my older brother and look for work there.

Eventually I found work in a timber yard. over the next eighteen months or so I worked hard all week and drank like a fish on the weekends and engaged with other risky activities with my mates. However, I eventually began to realise that this kind of lifestyle could not go on forever and that it was not one that could ever give me a meaningful future. I began to understand that I needed to do something different that might change my future prospects. Having recently got my driver's licence and bought a car one of my mates and I, made a plan to go over to mainland Australia and head west trying our luck in the mines. I gave my notice to the timber yard.

Then everything went a bit pear shaped when I was booked for drink driving. My licence was suspended for five months, and I copped a fine. The plan was not going to work anymore. However, I still wanted to change my circumstances. In the end plan B turned out to be move back in with the family in Victoria and maybe pick up my education.

The second plan ended up working quite well. I found a job in a sawmill within a week of arriving. Living with the rest of the family immediately began to change my lifestyle. No more excessive drinking or relying on cheap takeaway foods. I was even starting to save money. My social life, outside of work, also changed. Because it was part of the family routine I returned to church life again, attending Sunday worship and getting involved with the church youth group along with my younger brother and sister. This was despite my ambivalence about being Christian in a traditional sense.

Where does this ambivalence come from? I suspect it has a lot to do with my relationship with my stepfather. This relationship was not a simple matter. His marriage to my mother seems to have been much more a career move, than a 'love match'. He was young Methodist minister in his first full circuit placement. Back then in the early 1960s it was assumed that Methodist ministers would be married and that their families would also take leadership roles within the local congregation. By marrying a young widow with four children he would be able to fit the traditional Methodist minister image. We children were of course asked If we would be OK with this. However back in those times if adults asked children to ascent to some decision of theirs, we would understand the correct answer to the question was yes even if we had no real idea of the consequences. The same applies to our adoption and change of surname.

His personality was also very different to what we remembered of our father. When stressed he could explode into rage very easily. If we weren't constantly vigilant in reading his moods this violence could be directed at us. I took quite a bit longer than my siblings to get the hang of this vigilance. Consequently, I got far more than my share of thrashings for things I didn't know I had done. We lived with wariness around him. Decisions about life were clearly made by him for him rather than having much to do with what the rest of the family might want. These days we would recognise this controlling behaviour as a form of family violence or child abuse. However back then we all just normalised it.

While all of this is going on my stepfather also exposed me a much broader experience of the church and helped me to become a more critical thinker. There was exposure to the social justice ministry of the church. There were also warnings about the dangers of fundamentalist religion and an encouragement to read more serious books and even some theology. Topping the class at school and other academic achievements were valued and rewarded.

Because of this particular childhood background, as a young adult, I was probably better equipped to identify various different types of spirituality present in the local congregation. I was also wary of speaking out too much and causing concern to other members of the congregation. For the most part it was a fairly typical mainstream Protestant country congregation. The majority of the congregation would have held to a pre critical understanding of the scriptures. A few could have been described as fundamentalist in their understanding of the authority of the Bible. But there were also a few who were more liberal in their theology. For many of the congregation the social aspect of congregational life was much more significant than its theology. From my observation some in the congregation saw themselves as 'born again Christians' so would have been keen on evangelism. Others I could see were more pietistic where personal devotion was at the forefront of the various signs of Christian faith. Still others would have had a concern for 'traditional family values'. In many ways the faith of the congregation was still very much the same as had been true in Woorrady's time, a form of evangelical Christian monotheism. There seemed to be little here that could catch my imagination or give me the sense of meaningful purpose that could transform my still somewhat aimless life. However, in the winter of 1978 this was all about to change.

I had been a part of the youth Bible study group for about a year. This was the more serious core of the larger youth group. There were only six or seven of us along with the lay leader who led the group who was one of the 'born again' mob. He and the high school chaplain (a uniting Church minister) put together a weekend camp down in the Otway Ranges for our group. I can't recall exactly what passages the Bible studies were focused around. Most probably they included call narratives of prophets or disciples. Towards the end of the final session, we were encouraged to go off alone for a period of personal reflection. I wandered outside for it seemed that the rain had stopped although it was still overcast. As I wandered about thinking about what we had been discussing there was an opening in the clouds, a patch of blue could be seen. I looked up and suddenly it seems that there was a voice speaking in my head saying, 'Have you the courage to follow me?' If this was God, then it was certainly not the much narrower and perhaps tamer version I had been seeing in the local congregation. This was an altogether more robust God. One who recognised my wariness but also need for direction. How would I respond to his call, his challenge? Was I up for it? For this would surely set me apart. Yet here I was in just the sort of situation where I had always been open to my creator, amongst the tall trees, in nature, in creation. In faith and trust I had to say yes. And almost as an initial test, I had to go back inside when the group regathered and tell the story of this challenge and call.

Not long after this I came to the decision to return to Tasmania, to my own country. It seemed to me that the basic reason for me being in country Victoria, my need for direction and purpose in life had now been met. I needed a different context to continue the process of this call to discipleship. Within six months of my return, I had found a supportive Christian community in the congregation I had been part of during my high school years. It was a community that was much more open to dealing with young people with lots of theological questions. It was called the Hobart City Parish. It consisted of five congregations, three of which were large city churches and was led by a team of ministers, three of whom opened their homes on Sunday evenings for wide ranging discussions with a group of young adults, mainly university students.

Supported by this environment I had given up the sawmill work and enrolled at Elisabeth Matriculation College to finally get my university entry qualification. A retired pharmacist, who had been a leader of the Congregationalist Union in Tasmania, offered me cheap board in her home and I figured that my savings would get me through at least the first half of the year and that maybe I could get enough part-time or casual work to make it through.

I was still struggling with the direction that I should take beyond the end of the year. One option would have been to offer as a candidate for ordained ministry in the Uniting Church. I resisted this largely because I had grown up in a ministry household and was well aware of the potential downside of such a role. During the pre easter period of Lent the City Parish's evening service ran a special series of sermons on the theme of 'What my faith means for me'. Six speakers with quite different personal life stories, some lay and some ordained, were selected to deliver these sermons. They proved to be very popular. One of these speakers was the then Anglican Bishop of Tasmania. He spoke on the way the theme of 'challenge and response' had shaped his life of faith. His sermon resonated deeply with me as it recalled that sense of challenge that had been so significant for me that day in the Otway Forest.

Not long after this I found myself sitting in my minister's office taking about this, wondering if I did in fact have a call to ordained ministry. I think he was a bit ahead of me on this issue. After listening to me, he not only explained the process of selection and training for ordained ministry in the Uniting Church, but also asked me if I might take some services over the next six months on the east coast in a small rural parish that was too small to have its own minister. A bit of practical testing if you like. I agreed to this and, also to starting the selection process for ordained ministry.

On Pentecost Sunday 1979 I conducted my first solo service in Swansea. In the congregation was a retired minister, Rev Arwel Folkes-Williams, a sprightly seventy+ Welshman. Following the service, he took me on a long rambling walk and talk tour of the town. At the end of our walk, we arrived back at his unit. It was then that he took a book from his shelf and showed it to me. It was a copy of *On Being Christian* by Hans Küng. Arwel told me that it was the best book he had ever read on the subject of being Christian. He recommended that I get a copy and read it. Later that week I dutifully went to our local theological bookshop and bought a copy. This was my introduction to the theology of Hans Küng. It took me months to work my way through it. This was not so much because it was a thick book but because it was introducing me to new ideas and new words on almost every page. It had me getting up and going for a reflective walk section by section, and sometimes in response to a single sentence. The book proved to be an exciting new world for me. Five years later I had an opportunity to read his even longer book, *Does God Exist?* It only took five days! The difference that five years of tertiary study makes meant I could read it with understanding as I went. By this time, I was much more able to place myself within three–or four-thousand-year-old tradition of the discussion about

God. But I was probably not sitting within the middle of the spectrum of Christian belief and practice as were many of my contemporaries.

Having read Küng's book and some other theology during the year studying for my matriculation, I knew I need to do further theological education. At the time I had become candidate for ministry, the Uniting Church in Australia had only one pathway for which financial support could be gained. There was no Diaconate at that time. While there was a no fee policy for degrees from secular tertiary institutions and a reasonable government student allowance for undertaking such study, this was not available for theological degrees. The only way I could study theology was to be fully self-funded or as an accepted candidate.

As a person who was still relatively young and single, I was put on a six-year program. This involved two undergraduate degrees. The first was basically my choice in a secular university. The second would be in theology. As it happened, I had failed a first-year subject. The effect of this was to trouble the structure of my BA. I needed another first year subject to fulfil the requirement of a second major. A consequence of this was that instead of requiring one year to finish my degree it would take two years on apart time basis, for which there would be no student allowance. This situation was resolved by allowing me to move to Melbourne where I could finish my degree part time by doing agreed part time studies at the University of Melbourne for my Utas degree. At the same time be picking up some theology subjects and keep within the six-year timeframe. And be funded by the church student allowance.

Because of this arrangement I was probably the first part time candidate that the church had to deal with. While all the physical issues re a place to live on campus, finance and enrolments Melbourne Uni had been delt with, no arrangements had taken place regarding enrolments in the theological college. Apon arrival in Melbourne I went to see the dean of the UCA Theological Hall and asked about this. He was surprised and looked in his filing cabinet to discover who my course supervisor was. To his surprise his own name was on the card. I had arrived on the date given by the residential college for first time students, not knowing about pre-sessionals and the need to make arrangements to turn up a couple of weeks earlier. Candidates were usually expected to begin with the Pastoral Care pre-sessional. This was no longer possible. So, I was told to see the Dean of Studies for the United Faculty of Theology and enrol in Biblical Studies One. So, my time in theological studies started off as being something of an anomaly. Institutions tend to be a bit wary of these sorts of things. I was also one of only three theological students living in the residential college. All the others were either older married students or already living within commuter distance of the college. This tended to isolate the three of us from the rest of the student body and me even more so.

At the end of the first year while on my first field placement I also upset things a bit. This was also the summer of the Franklin River blockade in Tasmania. It was in the news a lot. Knowing that I was from Tasmania my supervisor for the field placement asked me about the blockade and discovered that I was all for it. Tasmania did not need this additional dam. He proceeded to offer to pay for my airfare on the basis that I would learn a great deal more participating in the blockade than I could ever learn working with him. I took the opportunity and went. I was arrested on the 6th of January and spent the next week in custody and later returned to the west coast base camp to train more blockaders. However, we failed to get permission for this alteration to my learning contract with the field education department. So, when I got back, I was sent back the Broadmeadows Parish mission for a further period of pastoral work. When a couple of other students who had also gone to the blockade after I had, were asked to talk to the student body about their experience, I was not included.

As it happened, I did not have at that time anything like a coherent theology to back up my actions. Eco Theology was not yet a thing so far as I knew. I just knew instinctively it was important to respect other parts of God's creation beyond the human. Articulating this in a theological way was still beyond me at that time. While I had been at theological hall for a year, I had only completed one full subject, Biblical Studies One in Old Testament. By the end of the following year the situation of being on the edge of things had improved markedly. I had finally finished all of the outstanding subjects of the arts degree and effectively what would normally be a full year of theological study which had included an introduction to the trinitarian theology of Jurgen Moltmann who was to be very influential in my theological development. I had also gotten married. This meant a greater degree of integration into the world of my fellow students. Two years later I had obtained my certificate of completion of studies and was able to proceed to Ordination.

Following ordination, I continued my theological education by completing a master's degree by research, on a part time basis while serving in rural placements. It was also the first real opportunity to have a go at exploring cross disciplinary approached to doing theology. In my undergraduate studies this had been rarely possible. The siloing of knowledge into separate disciplines had been the pattern. Yet I was often keenly interested in trying to see the whole through the relational connections between differing areas of knowledge. There was one exception to this pattern. The subject was Pastoral Studies Three. For this subject students were required to design a project where we would collect data from a series of interviews with a variety of different people. This data was then to be analysed both in terms of one of the social science disciplines, such as psychology or sociology, and theologically, in a major paper of 6,000 words. I was the only one in the group to get a distinction. All the others really struggled with this multi-discipline approach, yet to me this made instant sense. The assumption that all things are connected was coming to fore. This assumption was also to be part of my postgraduate studies, but I had to argue quite forcefully to be allowed to use this approach in my master's theses. The pattern in academia was still to stick within a single discipline rather than to explore it relationship to others.

The connection that we need to explore in this section is that between the aboriginal theology of Woorrady, discerned in the previous section, and Christian theology. The connecting theme that emerges in this context is that associated with the Wraerggowrapper-Moihernee dynamic through which the British invasion has been understood. From a western or mainstream perspective this theme is often called 'the problem of evil'.

Chapter 9
Wraerggowrapper—Philosophical and Scientific responses

The problem of Evil

As a philosophical problem the existential question of evil that is all too often experienced in our world not only includes the human against human evil that was the subject of the previous survey of twentieth century history but also the sense that we have of the unfairness, or randomness, of what we call natural evil. This includes premature death from illness, accidents, and natural disasters.

The philosophical argument on the Wraerggowrapper-Moihernee dynamic generally runs something like this,

> As a challenge to theism, the problem of evil has traditionally been posed in the form of a dilemma: if God is perfectly loving, he must wish to abolish evil; and if he is all-powerful, he must be able to abolish evil. But evil exists; therefore, God cannot be both omnipotent and perfectly loving.[1]

When presented in this way the Wraerggowrapper-Moihernee dynamic is only resolvable by either the denial of the reality of evil, or by making some adjustment to the notion of God presented here. While there may be some who are willing to deny the reality of evil, the vast majority of believers in God would not want to refute the existence of evil. Most of us have had more experience of evil in our world than we would wish.

We are left with needing to make some adjustment to the notion of God presented in the dilemma. In his article John Hick[2] goes in

---
1. Hick, 'The Problem of Evil', 126.
2. Hick, 'The Problem of Evil', 126.

this direction. He argues that even a God described in this manner, as 'omnipotent and perfectly loving' cannot be logically inconsistent. He therefore suggests that the world we have must be the best of all possible worlds. Hick then suggests that our world is the best of all possible worlds because it allows for the possibility of free moral choice.

There are some issues with this free moral choice argument. Firstly, the world we live in is the only one that we can know anything about at all. We may be able to imagine alternative possibilities, but we cannot have any confidence that any such alternative world might be better or worse than the one we do know. In his book, *Quantum Physics: Illusion or Reality*, Alistair Rae discusses the 'measurement problem' in quantum physics. In his chapter, 'Many Worlds', he discusses the 'many worlds' or 'branching universes' interpretation of this problem.[3] Apparently the mathematics of quantum events predicts two equally possible outcomes. So why not assume that both happen. On the very next page Rae writes,

> This leads us to an absolutely crucial point about the many-worlds interpretation: *once a split has occurred, the two branches have no way of being aware of each other.*[4]

While science fiction/fantasy writers may love the idea of many branching universes for the development of multiple plot lines they will have to invent magical or other means for the characters to get across this insurmountable communication barrier.

The second questionable issue is the use of the idea of being able to make moral choices as the basis for this world being the best possible world. Most of us would like to live in a world where the making of good moral choices was the general pattern, where we could trust each other to do the right thing much more often than often seems to be the case. A world where it was easy to do the right thing. However difficult moral choices seem to be very common. We are not all knowing so how do we make difficult decisions from a solid information base? Frequently we are also faced with time and resource constraints. We are not all powerful. Further, every situation is unique so it may not be ok to decide what to do on the basis of

---

3. Alistair Rae, *Quantum Physics: Illusion or Reality* (Cambridge: Cambridge University Press, 1986), 75.
4. Rae, *Quantum Physics*, 76.

what we did last time when faced with a similar situation. In some instances, we might find ourselves choosing between alternatives that feel like a choice between two evils. Sometimes the temptation to do nothing is strong, that, in itself, can have unwelcome consequences.

Hick's response to the Wraerggowrapper-Moihernee dynamic appears to be inadequate. Philosophical descriptions of God that basically take sets of human limitations and reverse them often feel inadequate. Our power is limited. God's is unlimited. Our knowledge is both limited and provisional. God is all knowing. We are capable of both good and evil, and of suffering both. God is all good and does not suffer. Another issue that arises with many philosophical descriptions of God is that God is made to seem a totally self-sufficient being. This can lead us to wondering why such a being would bother to create the world we know at all. What need has such a God for anything apart from itself? Perhaps what is needed here is some major change in the description of God, or a significantly different approach to the Wraerggowrapper-Moihernee dynamic.

Some years ago, I was attending a fiftieth birthday party for an old friend. When I noticed that another mutual old friend who I knew to be a lapsed Catholic, who understood himself to be a philosophical atheist, was eyeing me and drinking more heavily than I. Knowing him well I could sense that he was working up to an attack on my Christian faith. I waited patiently for it to come. When his opening question came it was in connection with the Wraerggowrapper-Moihernee dynamic, but its form was significantly different to the classic formulation. He proposed it in this way, 'If God created the world we know, he must have known that evil would exist and so he must have some responsibility for it.' I looked him in the eye for a moment and then answered, 'I could agree with that'. This was clearly not what he had expected. He was nonplussed and declined to reply. Unfortunately, we never got back to this discussion.

Why then, could I as a believer in God agree with my friend's statement? The answer lies in the manner in which the Wraerggowrapper-Moihernee dynamic was presented by my friend. He did not use the classic philosophical definition of God as the means of setting up the dilemma. This way of presenting the issue is sometimes known as protest atheism. This meant that other ways of understanding the nature of God might become applicable to the Wraerggowrapper-Moihernee dynamic as it is actually experienced in our world.

The way evil is actually experienced is sometimes described as human evil and natural evil. Traditionally natural evil included a fairly wide list. It included earthquakes, volcanic events, extreme weather events, outbreaks of potentially fatal disease, plagues of agricultural pests and so on. Just about anything over which human societies had little control. Human evil was about those things that we could control but failed to do so. Human on human violence in all its various forms. However, this distinction may not be as applicable as it once was. This is not only because developments in science and technology have given us many more means of mitigating the impact of natural evils on human societies but also because it is becoming clearer that human society now has a capacity to disrupt the ecological balance of the natural world in ways that puts all life on earth at risk. For example, the ever-increasing use of fossil fuels has warmed the atmosphere to the extent that extreme weather events are becoming both more frequent and extreme and therefore more damaging, effecting the very viability of some population centres.[5] It seems that there is a more complex story about the experience of evil here than the distinction between natural evil and human evil allows for. The real story may be much more interrelated.

A further issue with the Wraerggowrapper-Moihernee dynamic that needs to be noted is its unfairness. Evil seems to strike people in unfair and random ways. We might ask for example why this particular child was killed in a freak accident while a crime boss lives in luxury to a fine old age. We intrinsically feel that this sort of thing as incredibly unfair.

To get a better handle on both the interconnectedness of the experience of evil, and its unfairness. We will need to look at approaches to the subject of evil from a more contemporary perspective. One which seeks to approach the question from a scientific perspective and later in subsequent chapters one which gives a range of theological perspectives. This will require some understanding of differences in epistemology between these two disciplines.

---

5. See Chapter one above.

Quantum Uncertainty

Science uses what is called the empirical method. This will involve a hypothesis or new explanation of what is happening in the real world. The development of the hypothesis will frequently involve reason and mathematics that takes what is already known and extends it further looking for what might be possible as a more comprehensive explanation. This more comprehensive explanation is then tested. This may involve designing repeatable experiments and or the collection of data relevant to the issue in question. If those things that were predicted by the hypothesis are found to be the case, then this hypothesis is verified. This verification gives us more confidence that that the hypothesis is likely to be correct. If the experiment fails to verify the hypothesis, then it may need further theoretical modification and before further investigation. This whole process is about objectivity. It is about describing various aspects of the physical world as they actually are. It is worth noting that subjectivity is not entirely absent from the process. Frequently scientists will comment that in the process of developing a hypothesis that things like simplicity and elegance in the mathematics can sometimes be a guide towards the truth. So, there is some degree of subjectivity involved in the story.

Knowledge of the created world has expanded significantly since discussion of the problem of evil first began. Is there anything new that contemporary science can add to the conversation about the Wraerggowrapper-Moihernee dynamic?

During the twentieth century there were a couple of paradigm shifts in science's understanding of the world. In the seventeenth century Isaac Newton presented his laws of motion in doing so he was able to give a mathematical account of the movement of planetary and other celestial bodies around the Sun.

> Newton recognised that gravity also curves the paths of the planets around the Sun, in this case into ellipses. It was a great triumph that his laws of motion correctly described not only the shapes but also the periods of the planetary orbits. Thus it was demonstrated that even the heavenly bodies comply with universal laws of motion. Newton and his contemporaries were able to give an even more accurate and detailed account of the workings of the solar system. The astronomer, Haley for

example, computed the orbit of his famous comet, and was thereby able to give the date of its reappearance.

As the calculations became progressively more refined (and complicated) so the positions of planets comets and asteroids could be predicted with growing precision. If a discrepancy appeared, then it could be traced to the effects of some contributing force that had been overlooked. The planets Uranus, Neptune and Pluto were discovered because their gravitational fields produced otherwise unaccountable permutations in the orbits of other planets.

In spite of the fact that any given calculation could obviously be carried out to a finite accuracy only, there was a general assumption that the motion of every fragment of matter in the universe could in principle be computed to arbitrary precision if all the contributory forces were known. This assumption seemed to be spectacularly validated in astronomy, where gravity is the dominant force. It was much harder however, to test it in the case of smaller bodies subject to a wide range of poorly understood forces. Nevertheless, Newton's laws were supposed to apply to *all* particles of matter, including individual atoms.

It came to be realised that a startling conclusion must follow. If every particle of matter is subject to Newton's laws so that its motion is entirely determined by the initial conditions and the pattern of forces arising from all the other particles, then everything that happens in the universe, right down to the smallest movement of an atom, must be fixed in complete detail.[6]

By the nineteenth century it was becoming evident that this Newtonian paradigm was not a complete description of what actually happens in the universe. As successful as it is in describing the motions of relatively simple mechanics it is entirely without a sense of time. It appears to be describing a static universe. The Newtonian paradigm is just as successful at establishing position of planetary objects in the past as well as predicting their future. Because of the dominance of gravitational force in the solar system, changes over time are only

---

6. Paul Davies, *The Cosmic Blueprint* (Sydney: Allen & Unwin, 1989), 9–10.

likely to be measurable over incredibly long-time scales, over billions of years in length. The understanding of time here is effectively irrelevant to what happens, whereas we normally experience time as being unidirectional, that is travelling from the past into the future. The arrow of time as we experience it points in only one direction, the Newtonian paradigm has no real sense of time as we experience it. It is a steady state picture of the universe; a universe that essentially stays the same having no real development through time.

It is also a highly deterministic universe. What comes out of this is an unbroken chain of causation. A causes B, which in turn causes C and so on. Everything is caused by what goes before. In this universe all choices are in fact illusionary. This has us asking why we should bother trying to choose? Would it not be better to simply go with the flow and not stress about anything? Fatalism becomes the philosophy.

This might sound very depressing. One of Newton's laws concerned the conservation of energy. There is a toy called 'Newton's Cradle' which illustrates this. It generally consists of five identical steel balls each suspended from a frame by two strings of equal length. At rest all five balls rest against each other. If the end ball is swung out so as to swing back and hit the one next to it will be the one at the other end which moves while the middle three stay in place. Swing two balls out and the middle one stays at rest and the far two will swing out. This toy will keep up this back-and-forth process for a considerable period of time until friction against the air eventually slows it. In a vacuum this system would work ceaselessly. This small difference reveals a serious issue with Newtonian Physics. It is only in very special cases that it works effectively like the movement of planets around a star. When you factor in even very small additional variables, such as this dampening caused by air pressure, it doesn't work as a theory of everything.

What Davies is concerned with in his book, 'The Cosmic Blueprint', are two significant developments in twentieth century physics that indicate a dramatic shift away from the Newtonian paradigm. These shifts concerning the way we understand our universe, involve a divergence away from the earlier solid state and deterministic understanding. The first of these was through the development of quantum physics in the early part of the century and the second was the discovery of self-organisation in dissipative structures.

Paul Davies opens chapter 12 of *The Cosmic Blueprint* by writing,

> it is often said that physicists invented the mechanistic reductionist philosophy, taught it to the biologists and then abandoned it themselves. It cannot be denied that modern physics has a strongly holistic, even teleological flavour and that this is due in large part to the influence of quantum theory.
>
> When quantum mechanics was properly developed in the 1920s it turned science upside down. This was not only due to its astonishing success and explaining a wide range of physical phenomena. As with the theory of relativity which preceded it, quantum mechanics swept away many deeply entrenched assumptions about the nature of reality, and demanded a more abstract vision of the world.[7]

Here Paul Davies is telling us then when we consider quantum mechanics, we have to think about the world in quite a different way to the way we think about it on a day-to-day basis. To understand why it is helpful to quote him at length.

> Where quantum mechanics differs fundamentally from classical mechanics it is not so much in this 'one step removed' procedure than in the fact that the wave function only yields *probabilities* about observable quantities. For example, it's not generally possible, given the wave function, to predict *exactly* where a particle is located, or how it is moving. Instead, only the relative probabilities can be deduced that the particle is to be found in such and such a region of space with such and such a velocity.
>
> Quantum mechanics is therefore a *statistical* theory but unlike other statistical theories (e.g. the behaviour of stock markets, roulette wheels) it's probabilistic nature is not merely a matter of our ignorance of details; it is inherent. It is not that quantum mechanics is inadequate to predict the precise positions, motions, etc of particles; it is that a quantum particle simply *does not possess* a complete set of physical attributes with well-defined values. It is meaningless to even consider an electron, say, to have a precise location and motion at one and the same time.

---

7. Davies, *The Cosmic Blueprint*, 165.

> The inherent vagueness implied by quantum physics leads directly to the famous uncertainty or indeterminacy principle of Werner Heisenberg, which states that pairs of quantities (e.g. the position and momentum of a particle) are incompatible, and cannot have precise values simultaneously. The physicists can choose to measure either quantity, and obtain a result to the desired degree of precision, but the more precisely one quantity is measured, the less precise the other quantity becomes.
>
> In classical mechanics one must know *both* the positions and the momenta of all the particles at the same moment to protect the subsequent evolution of the system. In quantum mechanics this is forbidden. Consequently, there is an intrinsic uncertainty or indeterminism in how the system will evolve. Armed even with the most complete information permitted about a quantum system it will generally be impossible to say what the value of any given quantity (for example, the position of a particle) will have at later moment. Only the betting odds can be given.
>
> In spite of the indeterminism that is inherent in quantum physics, a quantum system can still be regarded as deterministic in a limited sense, because the *wave function* evolves deterministically. Knowing the state of the system at one time (in terms of the wave function) the state at a later time can be computed, and used to predict relative probabilities of the values that various observables will possess on measurement. In this weaker form of determinism, the various probabilities evolve deterministically, but the observable quantities themselves do not.[8]

Davies talks about quantum mechanics as a statistical theory. Clearly understanding something of what this means is important in getting a handle on the meaning of this last quoted paragraph and the 'weaker form of determinism' mentioned by Davies. We can do this by looking at a more familiar situation that is also statistically based.

In the eighteenth century the Church of Scotland had a serious pastoral problem that needed a solution. Being a protestant church clergy were permitted to marry. Renumeration for these clergy

---

8. Davies, *The Cosmic Blueprint*, 166–167.

and their families was managed in two ways. They were provided with housing and a stipend, or salary, to cover living expenses. Congregations or church institutions were expected to cover these costs. However, on the deaths of these clergymen these same resources would be required for the new incumbents. This often left widows, and any young children, with the double hit of homelessness and no reliable source of basic income. Significant numbers of widows of clergy were being left destitute following the deaths of their husbands. It was decided to create a pension fund for these women.

The problem to be solved here was how large did this pension fund have to be when it was impossible to know how long the widows would live beyond the deaths of their husbands. Some might live just a short time following the death of their husbands while other could live up to forty years or more to the event that their husbands died early due to misadventure of some kind. This is where statistical theory comes into the picture. The Church of Scotland was able to draw on some two hundred years of funeral records to gain statistical insight into the life expectancy of widows following the deaths of their husbands. This enabled an average figure for the period of time that the pension would have needed to cover had it been applicable in the past. It also gave an approximate figure for the future provided there was not a substantial change in circumstances. It also gave a figure for an annual contribution levy from Parishes and church institutions to fund the scheme.

However, it is important to note that averaging statistical data in this way does not tell us anything significant about particular individual circumstances. It is even possible that the average never actually happens except in a near approximation. It is frequently the case that future projections based on statistical data from the past can become less and less accurate the further into the future they are projected. This is why governments and other institutions call them "forward estimates" rather than determined outcomes.

Davies goes on to explain this 'hard to get one's head around' and apparently paradoxical behaviour quantum activity by reference to Niels Bohr's principle of complementarity.

> Bohr recognised that it is not paradoxical for electron to be *both* a wave and a particle because the wave-like and particle-like aspects are never displayed in a contradictory way in the

same experiment. Bohr pointed out that one can construct an experiment to display of the wave-like properties of a quantum object, and another to display its particle-like properties, but never both together. Wave and particle behaviour (and other incompatibilities, such as position and momentum) are not so much *contradictory* as *complementary* aspects of a single reality. Which face of the quantum object is presented to us depends on how we choose to interrogate it.[9]

If I understand all of this correctly then, when it comes to this sub-atomic quantum world, there is both an element of determinism and an element of freedom (indeterminism). To put it another way there is an interplay between chance and necessity within even in this fundamental level of physical reality. When it comes to our reflections on the Wraerggowrapper-Moihernee dynamic this introduces the idea that what we understand as evil is, at some level, intrinsic to creaturely existence. But also, of good. The element of freedom can go either way.

It is now time to turn to the second of Davies two twentieth century scientific revolutions: the discovery of self-organisation in dissipative structures.

Self-organisation

In the nineteenth century work was done on the efficiency of steam engines seeking better designs. This work led to laws of thermodynamics. It was the second law which turned out to be significant. Paul Davies in his book, *The Cosmic Blueprint*, describes it simply,

> Of these, the so-called second law of thermodynamics held the clue to the arrow of time. In its original form the second law states, roughly speaking, that heat cannot flow on its own from cold to hot bodies. This is, of course, very familiar in ordinary experience. When we put ice in warm water, the water melts the ice, because the heat flows from the warm liquid into the cold ice. The reverse process where heat flows out of the ice making the water even warmer is never observed.[10]

---

9. Davies, *The Cosmic Blueprint*, 167.
10. Davies, *The Cosmic Blueprint*, 15.

Davies goes on to describe it more precisely by introducing the concept of entropy.

> These ideas were made precise by defining a quantity called *entropy*, which can be thought of, very roughly, as a measure of the potency of heat energy. In a simple system such as a flask of water or air, if the temperature is uniform throughout the flask, nothing will happen. The system remains in an unchanging state called *thermodynamic equilibrium*. The flask will certainly contain heat energy, but this energy cannot do anything. It is impotent. By contrast, if the heat energy is concentrated in 'hot spot' then things will happen, such as convection and changes in density. These events will continue until the heat dissipates and the system reaches equilibrium at a uniform temperature.[11]

This second law of thermodynamics when applied to whole universe leads to the idea of the heat death of the universe. In this vision the universe will end when all energy in the universe has reached thermodynamic equilibrium, or maximum entropy. At that point nothing interesting can ever happen again. Even though such a vision maybe billions and billions of years in the future it is still something of depressing scenario. However, the very same law can also result in enormous creativity under some special conditions.

We will follow this thought as we move onto exploring a second paradigm shift in science towards the latter part of the twentieth century, the deepening understanding of complexity. In particular, there is a need to focus on the impact of the second law of thermodynamics in far from equilibrium systems.

Paul Davies writes,

> True scientific revolutions amount to more than new discoveries; they alter the concepts on which science is based. Historians will distinguish three levels of inquiry in the study of matter. The first is Newtonian mechanics—the triumph of necessity. The second is equilibrium thermodynamics—the triumph of chance. Now there is a third level, emerging from the study of far-from-equilibrium systems.[12]

---

11. Davies, *The Cosmic Blueprint*, 15.
12. Davies, *The Cosmic Blueprint*, 83.

Continuing Paul Davies notes that self-organisation occurs both in equilibrium and non-equilibrium systems. He then goes on to clarify a crucial difference between the two types of self-organisation.

> There is however a fundamental difference between the type of structure present in a ferromagnet and that in a convection cell. The former is a static configuration of matter frozen in a particular pattern. The latter is a dynamical entity, generated by a continual throughput of matter and energy from its environment: the name *process structure* has been suggested.
>
> It is now recognised that, quite generally, systems driven far from equilibrium tend to undergo abrupt spontaneous changes of behaviour. They may start to behave erratically, or to organise themselves into new and unexpected forms. Although the onset of these abrupt changes can sometimes be understood on theoretical grounds, the detailed form of the new phase is essentially unpredictable. Observing convection cells, the physicist can explain, using traditional concepts, why the original homogeneous fluid became unstable. But he could not have predicted the detailed arrangement of the convection cells in advance. The experimenter has no control over, for example, whether a given glob of fluid will end up in a clockwise or anticlockwise rotating cell.
>
> A crucial property of far-from-equilibrium systems that give rise to process structures is that they are *open* to their environment. Traditional techniques of physics and chemistry are aimed at closed systems near to equilibrium, so an entirely new approach is needed. One of the leading figures in developing this new approach is the chemist Ilya Prigogine. He prefers the term *dissipative structure* to describe forms such as convection cells . . .
>
> Organised activity in a closed system inevitably decays in accordance with the second law of thermodynamics. But a dissipative structure evades the degenerative effects of the second law by exporting entropy into its environment. In this way, although the total entropy of the universe continually rises, the dissipative structure maintains its coherence and order and may even increase it.

> The study of dissipative structures thus provides a vital clue to understanding the generative capabilities of nature. It has long seemed paradoxical that a universe apparently dying under the influence of the second law nevertheless continually increases its level of complexity and organisation. We now see how it is possible for the universe to increase both organization and entropy at the same time. The optimistic and pessimistic arrows of time can coexist: the universe can display creative unidirectional progress even in the face of the second law.[13]

To get a clearer understanding of what a dissipative system is it is helpful to look more closely at one of the simpler manifestations of this type of system. For this we will take a look at convection currents in water.

First let's set up the system. Take a pot and fill it with room temperature water and set it on the hot plate, but don't turn on the power just yet. It is important to note at this point that this simple physical system we had set up has boundaries which will impact on what happens as we go through the experiment. Liquid water will generally flow away to the lowest point, if not prevented. The Pot is an important boundary which constrains the water and whatever happens in it. The pot is not the only boundary condition. There is also an air pressure boundary on the surface of the water. If this experiment was attempted in a vacuum without the air pressure the liquid water would immediately start turning to gas as water vapour. This is also an important boundary condition. So, between the pot and air pressure the water is effectively a closed system in thermodynamic equilibrium.

Now let's see what happens when we turn on the heat. If we start with a very low amount of heat the results won't be particularly dramatic. What happens is the heat coming through the bottom of the pot simply warms the water slowly from the bottom towards the top. It does this by warming one layer of molecules at a time with this low level of energy input it will eventually reaching thermodynamic equilibrium throughout the column from bottom to top. It will be equally warm throughout.

So, next let's turn up the heat some more. At this point something incredible begins to happen. The energy flow is too great for the

---

13. Davies, *The Cosmic Blueprint*, 83–85.

molecule-to-molecule process of energy transfer to cope. Instead, convection cells spontaneously takeover. This might not sound all that incredible but to the physicist this sudden shift to higher level order in something as simple as liquid H_2O is remarkable as it involves millions of water molecules acting in concert to transfer energy throughout the system. Convection cells transfer energy from bottom to top in the water column. Between these upward moving convection cells heated water is moved to the top and cool water from the top is transferred to the bottom ready to be heated. This is a high efficiency and highly ordered process seeking to let the energy pass through while maintaining thermodynamic equilibrium throughout the bounded system.

It is important to understand some of the implications of this revolution in science around dissipative structures. Not only can they occur in fluid dynamics they are much more common in living systems. In fact, it seems that all living creatures on the planet, from the microscopic to the tallest trees, are dissipative structures. All of them interact in crucial ways with their wider environments. There is a constant flow through of energy and resources between all living creatures and their environments.

When it comes to living dissipative structures, it seems that the whole cannot be simply reduced to its component parts. Living entities exhibit patterns of behaviour and interaction with the environment it cannot be deduced from their chemical components. Simple reductionism, or what is sometimes referred to as nothing but-ism, cannot explain these qualities and behaviours. There is always a something more than biological chemistry going on.

Earlier when we were discussing Hick's notion of the world being the best of all possible worlds, we touched on an interpretation of quantum physics that envisaged a multiverse where a new universe splits off every time there is a quantum event. Now it is time to have a further look at the impact that quantum physics and dissipative structures has on our view of reality, in particular, with reference to chance and necessity.

In our exploration of the unfairness of evil as being intrinsic to the creative process of our universe we do not need to understand the detailed story of either quantum uncertainty or the interplay between randomness and necessity in complexity theory. What is needed here is sufficient understanding of these issues to see whether or not our decision making actually matters on the one hand, and on the other whether we must, to some extent, accept that some level of evil is intrinsically a product of the creative process of our universe.

Genetics—Do our Genes determine our future?

Elizabeth Finkel in her book, *The Genome Generation*[14] traces the story of genetic research from the first full reading of a human genome in 2001 up until the astounding results of the study of the coral genome. On the way she has included a chapter on a new area of biological science called epigenetics which means literally 'something above the genes'. One of the great hopes for the human genome project was that we would find specific genes that were responsible for a variety of medical conditions. This was achieved with a few very rare inheritable diseases. Faulty genes were found. However, in many more common chronic diseases such as diabetes and heart disease this did not prove to be the case. Instead, it became apparent that multiplicity of genes with complex interactions might be involved. Add to this a range of environmental and lifestyle factors that could also be interacting with the genetic story. It became clearer that for many common conditions something more was going on than the older idea that our genes were somehow deterministic of our future health.

Finkel's book also reveals some of the ways in which the old assumption that there was a relationship between the size and complexity of the genome and the complexity of the living being in question is not necessarily so. In the search for understanding the development of multicellular animals (roughly 600 million years ago according to the fossil record—before that we are talking about three billion years of single cell life). Finkel mentions three interesting examples of contenders for the title of basic level animals. These contenders are very similar to these early multicellular animals. Trichoplax, sponges and corals. However, all three of these have large complex genomes yet are very simple animals.

Trichoplax is only a millimetre or so wide an appears as flat smudge that slides over its prey and absorbs it. It apparently only makes use of five different cell types and so is very simple indeed. The Sponge

---

14. Elizabeth Finkel, *The Genome Generation* (Carlton: Melbourne University Press, 2012).

is similar although it has twelve types of cells. When their genomes were examined, it was a shock to discover how complex they were. Apparently, they have most of the genes it needed to make a brain, yet neither of them has a single brain cell.

Finkel follows the story of David Miller research into Coral DNA,

> Millar fully expected that the simple coral would possess a rather simple gene kit.
>
> It didn't. The rough reading revealed an unbelievable inventory of genes. Coral had genes that were supposed to be exclusive inventions of roundworms. It had genes that were supposed to be exclusive inventions of fruit flies. But, staggeringly, more than either of these two, the gene set it most closely resembled was that of a human being . . .
>
> Worse was to come. As more detailed versions of the coral genome were read, it started to reveal really bizarre stuff— things that didn't rightly belong to the animal kingdom at all. 'One set of genes jumped out and poked me in the eye,' Miller told me . . . Coral had a gene set that usually belonged to bacteria. It also had a set of genes that rightly belonged only to plants—the ones that give them their fruity smell. At first Miller didn't believe the findings. He suspected contamination out there on the moonlit reef who knows what might have contaminated his catch? . . . Yet year after year with each new coral spawn, Millar got the same result.[15]

How could all of this happen? It is known that before the advent of multicellular life that there was approximately three billion years of single celled bacteria and archaea colonising every corner of the planet. During this impressively long timeframe what is known as horizontal gene transfer where genetic material in imported into other cells by viruses or bacteria infecting them would also have been going on. Impressive collections of genetic material could have been building up waiting for an opportunity. About two billion years ago a larger single celled from of life emerged called the eukaryote which mastered the art of movement by evolving a fluid membrane, which also allowed it to engulf prey.

---

15. Finkel, *The Genome Generation*, 198–189.

Finkel tells us,

> The eukaryotic cell was a vastly improved model cellular life. Not only was it highly powered it cordoned off its genome in a membrane-bound nucleus to protect it from further invaders. eukaryotes came in several models. Some were hunters; some—the ones with chloroplasts—made their own food; some scavenged. Collectively, these single celled critters were called protists. Eventually they would give rise to the three kingdoms of multicellular life: animals, plants and fungi. But not for another 1.4 billion years!
>
> Many experiments were tried and failed in that long run up to multicellular life. Much of that period was probably spent honing a command and control system that would serve the needs of a complex society of cells.
>
> But even before our ancestor arrived on the scene many of the pieces were already in place. Archaea and bacteria had already invented ion channels to sense their environment. Those ion channels would pave the way for the development of nervous systems. Indeed some 27% of our genetic toolkit had already been evolved by kingdoms of archaea and bacteria 3 billion years ago . . .
>
> So perhaps it's little wonder that by the time the ancestor of animals made its appearance—a colony of hunter cells that found a way to hang together permanently—it was very well tooled-up. So well-tooled, that perhaps it could even afford to prune away some of its components in the course of subsequent evolution.
>
> It's hardly what we expected to find at the base of the evolutionary tree. But that's where reading genomes has taken us.
>
> So, meet your ancestor and be humbled: she was not much to look at but, on the inside, she carried a spectacular genetic dowry thanks to her three billion-year bacterial, archaeal and protest ancestry. By the time she arrived, most genes had already been invented. The 600 million years since then have just been variations on a theme.[16]

---

16. Finkel, *The Genome Generation*, 209–210.

In this biological story arising out of genomic research we again see an openness to the environment and complexity typical of dissipative structures. This story is also one that inclines us to see the whole as more than the parts. It is a fascinating story of creativity that cannot be reduced to it molecular components.

Looking at these examples from science it is becoming increasingly clear that our world is not a deterministic place. There are many systems operating that are indeterminate, where outcomes cannot be foreseen in advance. This is true of the quantum level, in dissipative structures and in genetics. It seems that there is both chance and necessity built into our universe. The creator's creation is full of surprises. Possibly even for its creator. It is however not possible for us to know the truth of this remark.

In his concluding Chapter of, *The Cosmic Blueprint*, Paul Davies introduces the idea of predestiny in contrast to the older idea of predeterminism.[17] The distinction between these two ideas if critical. Predeterminism belongs to the deterministic nature of the Newtonian paradigm or the teleological ideas of Aristotle. These ideas hold that everything in detail was laid down from time immemorial in an unchangeable way. Whereas predestiny lays down a pathway to self-organisation which is nevertheless not necessarily always achieved.

> It therefore leaves open the essential unknowability of the future, the possibility for real creativity and endless novelty. In particular it leaves room for human free will.[18]

One of the features of dissipative systems is their openness to the environment in which they exist. We encountered this idea earlier in a different form. The discussion of epigenetics presented in Elizabeth Finkel's book, *The Genome Generation*,[19] is also largely concerned with the way genetics is not deterministic. Outcomes are apparently much more often a result of the combination of genes and environmental factors.

It is also true that for every living thing there seems to be something that is happy to eat it to ensure its own survival. One of the factors that, it seems, still helps to drive this evolutionary process of life is

---

17. Davies, *The Cosmic Blueprint*, 197–203.
18. Davies, *The Cosmic Blueprint*, 201.
19. Finkel, *The Genome Generation*, Chapter 3.

competition for resources. For plants this is largely about space, light and soil. For animals it is about food supply. On a broad ecological level this is about finding different niches and strategies for living. However, on an individual level it can be very costly. With plants very few seeds will ever make it to maturity. In the animal world there are many examples where individual young do not make it. There is what we might describe an intrinsic unfairness within the creative process.

It seems I might have given an answer that was at least partly right to my protest atheist friend all those years ago. God does have some responsibility for the potential of random unfairness.

Chapter 10
Wraeggowraper—Biblical and Theological responses

Some Epistemological Matters

When we come to theology the epistemological story is somewhat different to that of science and even that of philosophy. Theology, which means the study of God. Rational thought is still important. But in addition, the category of revelation is also taken seriously. Revelation is basically the idea that from time-to-time God may decide to reveal something of God's nature to human beings. So, we have the term self-revelation. This can take many forms. Anything from sudden moments of enlightenment or insight, to dreams and visions, or even sudden or dramatic changes in circumstances. When it comes to the world's major religions much of this material may find its way into written documents which may be eventually elevated to the status of scripture. Examples of this are Hindu Upanishads, the Muslim Koran, the Book of Mormon, Buddhist sutras and, of course, the Bible. The authoritative nature of these scriptures may vary depending on the particular religious tradition they belong to. From an epistemological perspective these are not philosophical treatises or pieces of scientific empirical work. They are what we might call witness statements or testimonies. The Uniting Church in Australia in its Basis of Union, one of its foundational documents, has this to say about the Bible,

> The Uniting Church acknowledges that the Church has received the books of the Old and New Testaments as unique prophetic and apostolic *testimony*, in which she hears the Word of God and by which her faith and obedience are nourished and regulated.[1]

---
1. Paragraph Five, *The basis of Union*, Uniting Church in Australia, 1971 Italics—mine

As witness statements these documents will generally contain a good deal more human subjectivity than philosophical or scientific papers. There are a number of reasons for this. When describing an unusual event sometime later we may not remember all of the detail accurately. Few humans have photographic memories. We also tend to pick up most on those parts of events we are testifying about that affect us emotionally. Ludwig Wittgenstein's Duck/Rabbit, where a cartoon outline of a rabbit when rotated through 90 degrees looks like a duck, reminds us that two people might see something from different perspectives and interpret it meaning in quite different ways. If we are trying to get to the truth of some important matter on witness testimony alone it is helpful to have more than one witness. The more the better, as this allows us to see several perspectives and, importantly, notice common themes. Witness testimony can also be tested by cross examination, which also may allow the reliability of witnesses to be assessed.

When it comes to the Bible this cross examination of witnesses takes place in the world of biblical scholarship as a university discipline. The Bible is perhaps one of the most closely examined collection of texts in the world. In more recent post enlightenment times historical critical methods have been used to establish things like the date and historical context of the text in question, what can be said about authorship, literary genre, and style with reference to the ancient languages and surrounding cultures. With some of the different books of the Bible, when subjected to this critical scholarship, have also revealed traces of earlier source documents, serious editing, and reframing of older material. Sometimes this editing and reframing gives, what at first sight might be seen as a coherent whole, written by a single author in a relatively short time frame. It can turn out to reveal a whole much more complex and long-term development process.

Book of Job

It is now appropriate to return to the idea of God's responsibility for the evil we experience in the world. We will do this initially with a look at the Book of Job from the Hebrew Bible. The book of Job is not easy to date as it does not reference any historical events that can be otherwise verified. Instead, its dating has to rely on working out where it sits in terms the history of the development of Old Testament theology. Most scholars tend to locate it in the fifth century before the common era as it contests.

> the Deuteronomic doctrine of the rigid correlation of desert and fortune on the national scale ... It was probably under the influence of the application of this principle to the individual that the hard doctrine of Job's friends became accepted.[2]

It is generally thought to be from sometime about the end of the century, roughly 400 years before the common era.

It also needs to be noted that the book of Job nowhere seeks to resolve the Wraerggowrapper-Moihernee dynamic doling out reward, or punishment, in terms of an afterlife, or eschatologically as in the sense of a future judgement day, or end time event. Dating wise, this puts the book significantly before the book of Daniel where these ideas appear in the Old Testament for the first time. Daniel can be clearly dated to the middle of the second century before the common era.

The book of Job starts by introducing Job,

> There was once a man in the land of UZ whose name was Job. That man was blameless and upright, one who feared God and turned away from evil (Job 1:1a).

The ongoing description of Job makes it clear that he is an idealised character living the perfect life of a typical middle eastern patriarch. He has a large family, is wealthy with vast herds of livestock and many servants. He is even careful to offer special sacrifices just in case his children may have sinned. Then we get this extraordinary conversation in the court of God,

> The Lord said to Satan, 'Where have you come from?' Satan answered the Lord, 'From going to and fro on the earth, and from walking up and down on it.' The Lord said to Satan, 'Have you considered my servant Job? There is no one like him on earth, a blameless and upright man, one who fears God and turns away from evil.' Then Satan answered the Lord, 'Does Job fear God for nothing? Have you not put a fence

---

2. HH Rowley, *The New Century Bible Commentary—The Book of Job* (Grand Rapids: Eerdmans, 1980), 23.

> around him and his house and all that he has, on every side? You have blessed the work of his hands, and his possessions have increased in the land. But stretch out your hand now, and touch all that he has, and he will curse you to your face.' The Lord said to Satan, 'Very well, all that he has is in your power; only do not stretch out your hand against him!' (Job 1:7–12a)

Here we see God commissioning Satan to put Job to the test. What follows are a series of disasters, both natural and enacted by other humans. Job loses all his children, livestock and all his many servants with the exception of the sole survivors of each calamity who bear the news to him. Then in verse 20–22 we hear,

> Then Job arose, tore his robe, shaved his head, and fell on the ground and worshiped. He said, 'Naked I came from my mother's womb, and naked I shall return there; the Lord gave, and the Lord has taken away; blessed be the name of the Lord.' In all this Job did not sin or charge God with wrong doing.

So far Job has maintained his faith.

This is followed by a second conversation between God and Satan which ends by ramping up the test another notch. Job is afflicted with painful sores all over his body. At the end of this Job's wife suggest that he curse God and dies. He responds to her calling her a foolish woman and asks the question, 'Shall we receive the good at the hand of God, and not receive the bad?' (Job 2:10b)

After this Job's friends turn up and sit with him in silence for seven days and nights. A sign of solidarity and empathy. After this the main bulk of the book of Job (from Chapter 3 until chapter 42 verse 6) begins with a poetic speech by Job in which he curses the day he was born. There now begins a cycle of speeches where his friends try to discover a reason for his suffering based on some action or lack of action of Job's in failing to be free of wrongdoing. They basically do what today we would call blaming the victim. Job replies to each such speech by continuing to assert his innocence. Eventually he is driven to wanting to take his case against God to trial. God finally responds through a voice from the whirlwind. In doing so God shifts the framing of the conversation from justice and fairness, and from obedience to commandments, to the wonder of creation. Job's questions about justice and fairness are not answered. Yet at the same time his friend's theology that treats suffering as evidence of some sort of moral failing on the part of the individual sufferer is treated as ill conceived. While the application of the commandments, whether social or cultic, to the whole society may make some sense in maintaining equity and social cohesion as well as mitigating some evils, does not work so well when applied to particular individuals. At the individual level it often smacks of hypocrisy on the one hand and blaming the victim on the other.

The shifting of the frame of reference from individual fairness to the mystery of creation challenges us with a reminder that human knowledge is always incomplete, that there might be far more to the story than we can yet see.

At this point in the development of the Hebrew scriptures there is very little by way of ideas of an afterlife. The place of the dead is called Sheol.

> Throughout the Hebrew scriptures Sheol is regarded as a place of shadowy existence and certainly not a place of punishment. It is that cavernous region below the earth with the life force is no longer present and where personality no longer counts. In Sheol everything sheds its vitality.[3]

There is no significant change in this situation until the middle of the second century before the common era. At that time ideas of the resurrection of the dead begin to appear. This is a time of crisis for the Hebrew faithful in Jerusalem. Antiochus IV was the Seleucid Greek ruler of the region which included Jerusalem. He attempted to place his own statue in the temple and to enforce devotion to him as a god. This was highly offensive and regarded as blasphemy by many of the Jewish people. Most commentators agree that the Book of Daniel was written during this crisis and was intended to encourage the faithful. The final chapter of this book we read, "Many of those who sleep in the dust of the earth shall awake, some to everlasting life, and some to shame and everlasting contempt. (Daniel 12:2—NRSV) this idea is also present in 2 Maccabees chapter 7 in reference to the same crisis that faced the writer of Daniel.

The picture that arises from these ideas is one of general resurrection of the dead. All humanity will be present on judgment

---

3. Robert A Anderson, *Signs and Wonders* (Grand Rapids: Eerdmans,1984), 147.

day. It is in this context that the just and faithful ones will be rewarded while the wicked will be punished. These ideas were controversial even within the Jewish community. Some sects opposed them while others embraced them enthusiastically. This tension was still evident in the first century and is addressed by Jesus in the synoptic Gospels, where he favours the Pharisaic affirmation of the concept of resurrection in opposition to Sadducees who opposed it (Mk 12:18-27, Lk 20:27-40, Matt 22:23-33). The idea of judgement day and the general resurrection of the dead is also referenced in the synoptic Gospels. In Matthew 25:31-46 where the setting of the parable is judgement day. Although 'the sting in the tail' of parable is the suggestion that many of Jesus' listeners may have gotten the criteria for judgement quite wrong.

Putting off the Wraerggowrapper-Moihernee dynamic's resolution until judgement day does nothing to remove the reality of present pain and suffering for individuals. It only promises that there will be a resolution in terms of accountability at some time in the future. As such it prompts the cry of 'how long until the day comes?' This question is generally answered by, 'don't know'. Not an entirely satisfying situation.

Moltmann's Trinitarian theology of the Cross

Earlier when discussing some of the appalling things that we humans did to each other during the twentieth century I quoted Jurgen Moltmann's account of the impact that the revelation of Nazi atrocities had on him as a young prisoner of war. In that same little book about varieties of religious experience he goes on to tell us how out of that context he came to find hope. He tells us that that time he had grown up in a non-religious household but had been given in that prison camp a copy of the New Testament in the back of which included the copy of the Old Testament psalms. He goes on to say that was the psalms that lead him out of despair. He became fascinated by the poetry of the psalms. Reading this Hebrew poetry gently led him to hope again.

Some of these psalms have an emotional dynamic that begins with suffering and pain, anguish and despair are articulated, and God is questioned. These psalms can be deeply personal crying out for relief in the unfairness of life and yet end with doxology and praise. When I found myself a prisoner during the Save the Franklin River campaign as young man, I attempted to write a psalm of lament in the loneliness and powerlessness of my prison cell about how I was feeling at the time. What surprised me was that after giving full expression to a range of negative emotions about my situation and my fears about the possible success of our protest action in saving the river from being dammed, was that the last couple of lines of the poem turned to doxology and praise.

This dynamic is particularly true of Psalm 22, a psalm that was to become highly significant to Moltmann's theology. It begins with a cry of God-forsakenness, 'My God, my God, why have you forsaken me?' It then works through twenty-one verses of complaint, lament and fear before closing with 2 verses of praise and returning commitment to the God of Israel. Somehow the dynamic of this complaint and lament in conversation with God restores hope when there is no logical reason for hope.

It is important to note that the opening words of Psalm 22 are on Jesus' lips in the last moments before his death in the synoptic gospels, most starkly in Mark's gospel the earliest of the three. While following Mark, Matthew embroiders the death of Jesus with signs and wonders already anticipating resurrection and Luke adds a subsequent set of last words that soften the starkness of the cry of God forsakenness. He has Jesus say, 'Father, into your hands I commend my Spirit' (Luke 23:46b). Moltmann focuses his theology on Mark's account because it is not only earlier and therefore closer to the actual events in time, but also because of its very starkness. Being godforsaken and abandoned not only by friends and closest associates but also by the God whom he had called 'Abba' father. For all his life and ministry up until this final crisis Jesus' life and ministry has been marked by this intimate and uniquely close relationship with the God he understood as his loving father. Now in the moment of crisis, when it really mattered, that is broken.

We might also say here that God-forsakenness is another appropriate way of talking about how it feels when we are confronted with massive unfair evil, or Wrageowrapper let loose. Another way of following our broader theme.

In the 1970s Jurgen Moltmann's book *The Crucified God* appeared on the scene. At the centre of this book is an exploration of the theme god-forsakenness and abandonment within God. He chooses to work with this theme by developing a trinitarian understanding of God in attempting to understand the cross of Jesus from the perspective of the divine life. He attempts a God centric perspective.

From the fifth Century onwards the two natures of Christ and the trinitarian understanding of God are certainly reflected in the church's liturgy and are taught to the faithful on the basis the creed and Chalcedonian definition. However, their appropriateness to changing circumstances is not a discussion that is fostered by the institutional church. The Catholic theologian, Hans Kung sums up the situation from 451 to the 1970's quite well regarding the trinity,

> There is a story about a Bavarian parish priest who announced to his congregation on the Feast of the Trinity that this was so great a mystery, of which he understood nothing, that there would unfortunately be no sermon. Actually in both Catholic and Protestant churches sermons explicitly on the trinity are very rare.[4]

In *The Crucified God*, Moltmann attempts to understand the significance of the death of Jesus for God as Godself. Moltmann writes,

> When one considers the significance of the death of Jesus for God himself, one must enter into the inner-trinitarian tensions and relationships of God and speak of the Father, the Son and Spirit. But if that is the case, it is inappropriate to talk simply of 'God' in connection with the Christ event. When one uses the phrase 'God in Christ', does it refer only to the Father, who abandons him and gives him up, or does it also refer to the Son who is abandoned and forsaken? The more one understands the whole event of the cross as an event of God, the more any simple concept of God falls apart. In epistemological terms takes so to speak trinitarian form. One moves from the exterior of the mystery which is called 'God' to the interior, which is trinitarian. This is a revolution in the concept of God which is manifested by the crucified Christ.[5]

---

4. Küng, *Does God Exist?*, 699.
5. Jürgen Moltmann, *The Crucified God* (London: SCM Press, 1974), 204.

Moltmann writes this passage in the context of a longer piece that critiques the theology of the cross since the time of Luther in the Reformation. He points out that for a long period the theology of the cross had been focused on how the death of Jesus applied to human beings. In other words, the focus was on soteriological, or salvific, importance of Jesus death in regard to the forgiveness of sins and the possibility of salvation. He is changing the perspective from what Jesus' death means for human beings to what it might mean for God, and so what it might tell us about the creator creation dynamic. Moltmann goes on to say,

> the death of Jesus on the cross is the *centre* of all Christian theology. It is not the only theme of theology, but it is in effect the entry to its problems and answers on earth. All Christian statements about God, about creation, about sin and death have their focal point in the crucified Christ. All Christian statements about history, about the church, about faith and sanctification, about the future and about hope stem from the crucified Christ. The multiplicity of the New Testament comes together in the event of the crucifixion and resurrection of Jesus and flows out again from it. It is one event and one person. For cross and resurrection are not facts on the same level; the first expression denotes a historic al happening to Jesus the second an eschatological event. Thus the centre is occupied not by 'cross and resurrection' but by *the resurrection of the crucified Christ* which qualifies his death as something that has happened for us, and *the cross of the risen Christ* which reveals and makes accessible to those who are dying his resurrection from the dead.[6]

This is a complex quotation. Talking about the crucifixion and resurrection of Jesus Moltmann is affirming that this is one event and one person. Crucifixion and resurrection need to be held together for the significance of both to become apparent. The death of Jesus needs to be understood as real prior to any meaningful understanding of resurrection. He is also right to distinguish between crucifixion and resurrection saying they are not on the same level and to then point out that Jesus' death is something that happens historically for our sake, while Jesus' resurrection is the source of our hope and

---

6. Moltmann, *The Crucified God*, 204.

the hope of all creation. Without this double understanding of this one event both the cost of death for God and creation and the hope of new creation and the future of the indwelling of God through eschatological transformation would not be realised. Death and the story of suffering creation must be taken up into Godself so that resurrection life may become real for both God and the completion of creation.

Earlier in his book Moltmann examines different understandings of God in religion, theistic philosophy, and atheistic philosophy. He finds most of them to be inadequate in the face of unfair suffering. The one that he regards as having some credibility is what he calls protest atheism. This is atheism that arises out of a critical awareness of the randomness and unfairness of so much of the suffering we see in the world. The complaint of Job is a legitimate response to such suffering.

> The only way past protest atheism is through a theology of the cross which understands God as the suffering God in the suffering of Christ and which cries out with the godforsaken God, 'My God why have you forsaken me?' For this theology, God and suffering are no longer contradictions, as in theism and atheism, but God's being is in suffering and the suffering is in God's being itself because, God is love. It takes up the 'metaphysical rebellion' up into itself because it recognises in the cross of Christ a rebellion in metaphysics, or better, a rebellion in God himself: God himself loves and suffers the death of Christ in his love. He is no 'cold heavenly power' nor does he 'tread his way over corpses', but is known as the human God in the crucified Son of man . . .[7]

Moltmann continues his trinitarian analysis of the cross of Jesus,

> Paul introduces a radical change in the sense of 'deliver up' when he recognises and proclaims the godforsakenness of Jesus in the eschatological context of his resurrection rather than in the historical context of his life. In Rom. 8.31f., we read 'If God is for us, who is against us? He who did not spare his own Son but gave him up for us all, will he not also give us all things with him?' According to this God gave up his

---

7. Moltmann, *The Crucified God*, 227.

own Son, abandoned him, cast him out and delivered him up to an accursed death. Paul says an even stronger terms: 'He made him sin for us' (II Cor 5.21) and 'He became a curse for us' (Gal 3.13). Thus in the total, inextricable abandonment of Jesus by his God and Father, Paul sees the delivering up of the Son by the Father for godless an godforsaken man. Because God 'does not spare' his Son, all the godless are spared. Though they are godless, they are not godforsaken, precisely because God has abandoned his own Son and has delivered him up for them. Thus the delivering up of the Son to godforsakenness is the ground for the justification of the godless and the acceptance of enmity by God. It may therefore be said that the Father delivers up his Son on the cross in order to be the Father of those who are delivered up. The Son is delivered up to this death in order to become the Lord of both the dead and the living. And if Paul speaks emphatically of God's 'own Son', the not-sparing and abandoning also involves the Father himself. In the forsakenness of the Son the Father also forsakes himself. In the surrender of the Son the Father also surrenders himself, though not in the same way. For Jesus suffers dying in forsakenness, but not death itself; for men can no longer 'suffer' death, because suffering presupposes life. But the Father who abandons him and delivers him up suffers the death of the Son in the infinite grief of love. We cannot therefore say here in patripassian terms that the Father also suffered and died. The suffering and dying of the Son, forsaken by the Father, is a different kind of suffering from the suffering of the Father in the death of the Son. Nor can the death of Jesus be understood in Theopaschite terms as the 'death of God'. To understand what happened between Jesus and his God and father on the cross, it is necessary to talk in trinitarian terms. The Son suffers dying, the Father suffers the death of the Son. The grief of the Father here is just as important as the death of the Son. The Fatherlessness of the Son is matched by the Sonlessness of the Father, and if God has constituted himself as the Father of Jesus Christ, then he also suffers the death of his Fatherhood in the death of the Son. Unless this was so the doctrine of the Trinity would still have a monotheistic background.[8]

---

8. Moltmann, *The Crucified God*, 242–243.

This is a rather long quotation but an important one as it gets to the very heart of Moltmann's theology of the cross. However, despite this the care which is taken to bring out the suffering of both Father and Son there appears to be no mention of the Holy Spirit in this exposition, or is there? So how is this a trinitarian theology?

A key term in this theology of the cross is God-forsakenness. It is here that we find the Holy Spirit, or rather the absence of the Holy Spirit. Throughout his ministry Jesus is depicted as one who is not only intimately related to the God, he calls Father, but also as one who is uniquely empowered by the Holy Spirit for the ministry he is about to start. The Synoptic gospels point to this with the baptism by John during which the spirit of God descends on Jesus and the voice of God blessing him. John's gospel makes John the Baptist declare that Jesus is the one who is to come and who will baptise with the Holy Spirit. Jesus' ministry is seen by all four gospels as Spirit-filled. The Spirit, or breath of God, is seen as the connectedness to the life of God. God-forsakenness means that this connectedness to the life of God is broken. In the theology of the cross Jesus and the God he called father have lost this connection in the absence of the Holy Spirit they are isolated from each other and suffer the loss of their relational intimacy.

There are two things that we can take from this trinitarian Interpretation of the cross. First, God's empathy for those who suffer. In the cross of Jesus abandonment, pain and suffering enter the very heart of God threatening the foundations of God's own self designation as love. So, we can say that the experience of abandonment pain and suffering, the very experience that all creatures can suffer, is both felt and known at the centre of God's own being. In this way we can understand God's empathy for all creation, Including us, in our suffering. We can also be aware of God solidarity standing with us in our suffering. Despite the way it may feel, we are not alone.

Second, a summons to resist and mitigate evil and suffering wherever we can. If we recall how it came to be that Jesus suffered this kind of death, one that was not only extremely painful but also meant to humiliate and show him as accursed, we can see that this is also a political death. It is often noted, particularly in the synoptic gospels, that throughout his ministry Jesus has a bias for the poor, the outcast and the stranger expressed in his teaching and actions. The sick are healed and returned to community, the rich and powerful are criticised and community leaders are warned about their hypocrisy in touting righteousness while ignoring the poor. Jesus' ability to attract crowds becomes a political problem. In this context the powerful decide he needs to be removed. However, he is not a violent rebel or dangerous criminal. The powerful in the Jewish community will need to convince the Roman authorities that he is a danger to public order. Crucifixion is for escaped slaves and rebels who undermine Roman authority. So, his is a political death as well. Jesus challenged social conditions that pushed some, particularly the poor and outcast, towards a less than human existence, while at the same time allowed others privileged access to power. This makes his death a summons to those who follow him to also advocate for social and environmental change in solidarity with the powerless.

Where have we Travelled so Far in this Section?

This section began with an account of world history from the time of Woorrady to the present day. This account concludes with the assessment that the Wrageowrapper designation the nature of mainstream society is still applicable and in fact seems to have intensified. We followed this by looking at the themes of 'the problem of evil' and 'protest atheism' in philosophy and science.

In doing so we noted that the philosophical discussion on the presence of evil began with a notion of God that has its origins in Greek philosophy. This idea of God defines God in terms of being all powerful, all knowing and all good. If defining God in this way is correct, then one must argue that this world is the best of all possible worlds because it allows an element of free moral choice. Then asserting that even this God could not logically do better. This line of argument does not seem fully convincing, especially because it does not give a reason why such a God would bother to create at all or why 'moral choice' should be valued above all else in this way.

In examining twentieth century scientific advances we saw that far from being deterministic two major discoveries revealed elements of freedom in the way the universe works. On the subatomic level there is the wave particle duality which leads to the uncertainty principle. The second arises out of far from equilibrium thermodynamics in dissipative systems. These can lead to spontaneous development of ordered behaviour on a macro scale in physical systems and in biological systems even seen to exhibit top-down causation. Both suggest that there is an interplay between freedom and necessity such that outcomes cannot be determined in advance. And that this means that there is always going to be in creation, as we know it, some degree of unfairness that must be lived with.

We also saw that there is enormous potential for creativity in living dissipative systems. Recent work on genetics reveals that even comparatively simple life forms such a sponges carry with them all the genetic coding to construct something as complex as a human brain. So, it seems that the unfairness in the creation may be related to this enormous potential for creativity.

We then went on to look at biblical and theological responses to 'protest atheism' in the Old Testament and in Moltmann's trinitarian theology of the cross. While these do not eliminate the unfairness, particularly for individuals, divine empathy and solidarity with suffering is affirmed.

So far, the wraerggowrapper designation is still with us and is not likely to be eliminated while this creation lasts.

It is now time to turn our attention to the radical insight that the crucified Jesus has been raised from the dead and to see where that leads.

Chapter 11
Resurrection and New Creation

Beginning with Paul

In recent years I have been much helped in my understanding of the resurrection of Jesus. A small book by the New Testament scholar, Bernard Scott called 'The Trouble with Resurrection'[1] has been particularly helpful in this process. In his book Scott, begins with and encouragement to see this theme in terms of the chronological development of resurrection within the New Testament. This means starting with Paul's letters rather than the later gospel accounts. Paul was writing from the late 40s well into the 50s. This makes him apart of the first generation of the church. Whereas the earliest gospel, Mark, is generally dated at about 70 CA, with the other three gospels having dates between the late 1st century impossibly even into the second century. Scott is concerned that we are not drawn into reading back into Paul's letters accounts of the resurrection from the much later gospels. He is also concerned to prevent us seeing Paul's shift from opposition to the new faith to becoming an advocate for it through the lens of the Acts story of his Damascus Road experience. Instead, we should first look at what he has to say about it for himself in his letters. Scott is concerned that the long-established format of the New Testament, starting with the Gospels and then Acts before we get to Pauls letters, together with the church's tradition of using the New Testament liturgically, where the Gospels have a much greater prominence, also tends to lead to us reading later accounts back into the letters.

---

1. Bernard Brandon Scott, *The Trouble with Resurrection* (Salem: Polebridge Press, 2010).

There are two occasions when Paul talks about his experience of the resurrection, or more properly the experience that turned him from trying to wipe out this new Jesus movement towards becoming an apostle/envoy for it. In both of these passages Paul is defending his apostleship and importantly the core of the message that he had preached. The first of these occasions is found in the first part of the letter to the Galatians. The second is found in chapter 15 of the first letter to the Corinthians.

If we follow Scott and treat Paul's accounts as primary eyewitness testimony, as opposed to the Acts account as both secondary and significantly later, we might well begin to wonder whether the Acts account has much connection with Paul's actual experience. Scott points out that as Jew of the Pharisee party he was already a believer in the Biblical God so there is no need of conversion from one religion to another. Instead, he suggests that Pauls experience seems to be much closer to Prophetic call narratives in the Old Testament; in particular those of Isaiah and Jeremiah. There are some biographical elements in these passages that do not fit easily into the Acts story. In the Acts story Paul is on his way to Damascus with letters of authority from the leaders of the Jewish community with the object of preventing the development of the Jesus movement in that city on the way he has a very dramatic vision and is temporarily blinded. This is followed up with some teaching about the gospel resulting in baptism into that community. This is a classic conversion narrative like others by the author of Luke/Acts. Both the Emmaus story and Philip's conversion and baptism of the Ethiopian official also place teaching from the scriptures before conversion. Paul, in his accounts is adamant that his proclamation has directly come from God; that it is a matter of revelation from God and is not in any sense a result of human teaching.

Paul is well aware of the epistemological vulnerability of his stance, when insisting on the revelatory nature of the message he proclaims. In in the opening chapter of the first letter to the Corinthians he says,

> Where is the one who is wise? Where is the scribe? Where is the debater of this age? Has not God made foolish the wisdom of the world? For since, in the wisdom of God the world did not know God through wisdom, God decided, through the foolishness of our proclamation, to save those who believe. For Jews demand signs and Greeks desire wisdom, but we

> proclaim Christ crucified, a stumbling block to Jews and foolishness to the Gentiles, but to those who are the called, both Jews and Greeks, Christ the power of God and the wisdom of God. For God's foolishness is wiser than human wisdom and God's weakness is stronger than human strength (I Cor 1:20–25).

In the letter to the Galatians as part of his defence of his apostolic calling Paul does add some biographical details.

> For I want you to know, brothers and sisters, that the gospel that was proclaimed by me is not of human origin; for I did not receive it from a human source, nor was I taught it, but I received it through a revelation of Jesus Christ.
>
> You have heard, no doubt, of my earlier life in Judaism. I was violently persecuting the Church of God and was trying to destroy it. I advanced in Judaism beyond many among my people of the same age, for I was far more zealous for the traditions of my ancestors. But when God, who had set me apart before I was born and called me through his grace, was pleased to reveal his Son to me, so that I might proclaim him among the Gentiles, I did not confer with any human being, nor did I go up to Jerusalem to those who were already apostles before me, but I went away at once into Arabia, and afterwards I returned to Damascus.
>
> Then after three years I did go up to Jerusalem to visit Cephas and stayed with him for 15 days; but I did not see any other apostle except James the Lord's brother. In what I am writing to you, before God, I do not lie! Then I went into the regions of Syria and Cecilia, and I was still unknown by sight to the churches of Judea that are in Christ; they only heard it said, "The one who formerly was persecuting us is now proclaiming the faith he once tried to destroy." And they glorified God because of me.
>
> Then again after fourteen years I went up again to Jerusalem with Barnabas taking Titus along with me. I went up in response to a revelation. Then I laid before them (though only in a private meeting with acknowledged leaders) the gospel that I proclaim among the Gentiles, in order to make sure I was not running, or had not run, in vain (Galatians 1:11–2:2).

The biographical information in this passage is quite sparse. There is the three years in Arabia and Damascus. Paul says nothing about what he was doing during this time. We might assume he was preparing for his new calling as an apostle to the Gentiles by reviewing his already significant knowledge of God as zealous Jew of the Pharisaic tradition in the light of his revelatory insight.

Paul does tell us about his two visits to the leaders of the Jesus movement based in Jerusalem. Initially a visit of fifteen days staying with Cephas (Peter) during which he also met with James the Lord's brother. Both of these men were key leaders of the early Christian movement. He does not tell us what they discussed on this occasion. However, we can assume that there were at least two matters that they discussed. Firstly, we can assume that they talked about the revelation that they received that Jesus, who was crucified, was alive and whose living and dying was a revelation of and from God whom Jesus called 'abba', father. This would be a touching base on the core insight that they had received. In connexion with this early Christian situation Scott puts forward a hypothesis. He reminds us that before Jesus' crucifixion the group surrounding him had experienced the way Jesus lived acted and expressed a radical vision of God. This included ministry of healing, release from demons, the gracious forgiveness of sin and acts of compassion. In doing so Jesus liberated people, particularly those on the margins of society, restoring them to community, freeing them from oppressive burdens, and acknowledging their dignity as persons. At the same time, he challenged the rich and powerful. Jesus also gave through his words and actions people a new vision of God. Instead of God a God who was like an emperor writ large Jesus presented God as a loving father who valued everyone, all of his creation with love and grace, creating hope and wonder. The remarkable thing was that this radical change of perspective was still breaking out amongst those who had followed Jesus, even after his death by crucifixion. This led to the idea that in some sense Jesus was alive and that they, as believers, also participated in this resurrection life. Scott reminds us that Paul, Peter and James were Jews deeply steeped in the Pharisaic understanding of the general resurrection of the dead and so if Jesus was alive then they also were participating in his resurrection life as signified by the continuing liberation begun in Jesus.

Second, we might also assume that there was some discussion about the mission to the gentiles. Included within the Old Testament scriptures that these early leaders shared was the idea that part of the purpose by God for the people of Israel what's that they should be a 'light to the gentiles'. That in some sense the understanding of God in Judaism at some point needed to be taken to the other nations surrounding the people of Israel. Being a diaspora Jew, having grown up in a gentile city, Paul felt that this was a task he should take up. Peter and James may well have acknowledged Paul's greater capacity to take the message of Jesus into the Greco-Roman context and so were willing that he should be an apostle to the gentiles.

The word apostle comes from the context of diplomacy and means something like special envoy. When it comes to this understanding of the role of such apostles, we need to note that the focus ought not to be placed on the individual as apostle/envoy but on the message being conveyed. This means that Paul, when defending his apostleship, does not want to stand on his own authority. Rather he is concerned for the authenticity of the message. This is why he insists on the message as being a revelation from God.

In chapter 15 of the first letter to the Corinthians Paul picks up the theme of resurrection. He does this initially by referring to the core of the message that he preached to them.

> For I handed on to you as of first importance that I in turn had received: that Christ died for our sins in accordance with the scriptures, and that he was buried, and that he was raised on the third day in accordance with the scriptures (I Cor 15:3–4).

Paul then goes on to list others who have received what basically seems to be the same revelation. He talks about there being 500 witnesses in all. While he does not list all the names, he does include most of the recognised leaders of this first generation of believers. He includes the 'twelve', Cephas (Peter), James the brother of Jesus and finally himself. Traditionally we tend to think in terms of twelve apostle, but this list has already got fourteen. Luke—Acts replaces Judas with Matthias, then add James and Paul. This is not to say that all 500 had exactly identical experiences, but rather that they all have had transformative revelatory insights that pointed to the crucified Jesus as the living one. Nor is it to say all 500 were apostles but that those who were commissioned to take this new revelation to other communities could be understood as apostles in the same sense that Paul, James and the twelve understood this form of ministry.

This revelatory experience amongst those who already accepted the earlier Jewish notion of the general resurrection of the dead, on some future judgement day, naturally leads to the conclusion that Jesus has been raised from the dead. Although Jesus' resurrection has already happened in anticipation of that future day. Also, because the earlier notion of general resurrection is corporate in nature if Jesus is alive then the believer also lives through participation in Jesus' life. This is how it is possible for Paul to say, 'I have been crucified with Christ; and it is no longer I who live, but it is Christ who lives in me' (Galatians 2:19b–20a).

Scott summarises his extensive discussion of the Pauline material in the following passage,

> Paul's view of the body raised up from the dead his critical to an understanding of his view on resurrection. From this discussion we can draw a number of conclusions:
>
> - God raises up the dead.
> - Paul rejects the immortality of the soul.
> - Humans (and animals, etc., for that matter) are bodies.
> - The body that God raises up or transforms is not a soul-body, it is not flesh and blood.
> - The body that God raises up is a new body that has God's breath as the principle of life.
>
> Beyond this Paul does not speculate. He does not answer some of the questions that we may have. Paul thinks in terms of an apocalyptic model. The basics of that model did not change from when he was a pharisee to when he was an Anointed-believer. What changed was the timetable. God had acted now by making the crucified Jesus his son and his anointed. This was demonstrated by God's raising him from the dead. This resurrection is the first step, the first fruits, in a scenario that will result not only in the raising up or transformation of all those who are Anointed-believers, but also in the reclaiming of creation—all will be made subject to God. This explains the first and second Adam language, as well as the language of a new creation.
>
> What Paul says about the body God will raise up also applies to the body of the Anointed. It is a soma pneumaticon, a body in which God has breathed God's life. This description of the

> body coheres with how Paul has employed 'he has been seen for/by' and 'God revealed in his son to/in me'. As a body in which God has breathed life, it cannot be seen by the eyes of flesh and blood, but can be seen only as made manifest by God. When Paul says, 'I have seen the Lord', that is what he means. The Lord is a soma pneumaticon, a body in which God has breathed God's life. For Paul a flesh and blood Jesus would not be addressed as 'Lord' or 'son of God'. Only as raised up from the dead is he Anointed, lord, and son of God. This explains why there are no appearance stories in Paul. For Paul it is not an event that can be shaped in that way.[2]

In the above passage Scott comments that what had changed in the understanding of the resurrection of the dead from the pre-Jesus pharisaic understanding was the timing. However, this is not the only thing that changes in the general resurrection of the dead scenario. What also changes is the criteria of judgement. There is a shift away from compliance with both the social and cultic legislation of the Torah. In Paul's later letter to the Romans, he works through a lengthy argument Regarding salvation by faith. Paul is arguing the case for being judged righteous because of faith rather than by works. He deliberately takes Abraham as his example rather than Moses. In doing so he is choosing someone who predates the giving of the law. In Paul's understanding of Old Testament history God's promise to Abraham about becoming the father of nations when he is already old without an heir and Abraham's trust in this promise makes him an exemplar of faith in God and therefore righteous. In Matthew's gospel we also see an illustration of this change of criteria. In Matthew chapter 25: 31–46 we have the parable, commonly known as 'the sheep and the goats'. The scenario here is the general resurrection of the dead for judgement. In this parable it is not compliance with the law what is the criteria of judgement but rather heartfelt acts of compassion towards those who suffer. Such acts are valued as though they were done for the one who judges, Jesus the human one. The criteria of the judgement are not legalistic but Christlike behaviours born out of trust in the way of Jesus.

The shift in timing and the change in the criteria of judgement also lead to a shift in eschatological understanding. Instead of a single

---

2. Scott, *The Trouble with Resurrection,* 141–142.

event at the end of time we now have the breaking in of the future in the present as signs of the eschatological consummation to come.

Resurrection Accounts in the Gospels

So far, we have been mainly concerned with the Pauline material on resurrection. There is of course further resurrection material in the New Testament. All the gospels have resurrection narratives following Jesus' death. What can be said about these witnesses to resurrection?

There are a few things we need to note about the gospels before we inquire into what the four gospels have to contribute to the discussion on resurrection. The scholarly consensus is fairly solid with respect to dating Mark's gospel as the earliest. It is generally dated as having appeared around 70 AD. This date is towards the end of the first Jewish war against the Romans. This war was devastating for the Jewish community in Palestine. It included large scale destruction in Jerusalem including almost total destruction of the temple. Several factions in Judaism that were based in Palestine or were associated with the Jerusalem temple, either disappeared altogether or suffered serious decline. Synagogue based tradition, which was also part of the wider diaspora, along with Pharisaic and rabbinic teachings, emerged as survivors as did the gentile church. It is thought that most of the leaders of the early Christian movement died during this time. Tradition holds that both Peter and Paul were executed in Rome at this time. The Romans probably regarded them as leaders of just another potentially dangerous Jewish sect. This war and the deaths of key leaders may well have been a factor in need to write down the story of Jesus for the emerging second generation of the Christian movement.

Over the next couple of decades, we see both Matthew and Luke's Gospels appearing. Both are heavily dependent on two sources. The Gospel of Mark is extensively quoted word for word by Matthew and Luke and, at some points, with minor changes of wording. Some of this Marken material is placed differently to the original in the overall narrative by Mathew and Luke. This is reflective of the different theologies of Matthew and Luke. There is also a significant body material that is common to both of these two gospels that is not from Mark. This is known as the Q source. It largely consists of teaching material from Jesus. The Lord's prayer and large parts of the sermon on the mount come from this source. This source, as far as we know does not contain a passion narrative or any resurrection material. It is only known at all through its use by Matthew and Luke. No original has been found. It may have been much more extensive; we simply don't know. Some scholars suspect it may have been compiled by a group who saw Jesus as a true prophet and so were concerned to preserve his teaching.

John's Gospel was probably the last of the four to appear in the very late first century or even early in the second century. Any reader of John's Gospel will notice that it is very different to the other three in both style and theology. It clearly represents a different tradition to the others. The prologue of John's Gospel (first 14 verses) sets up the story of Jesus as having cosmic significance; styling Jesus as the incarnation of the divine word. There are also the "I am" sayings which echo the revelation of the divine name to Moses at the burning bush in Exodus. Throughout the Gospel Jesus always seems in control of his own destiny, even during his trial and passion. There is none of Mark's god forsakenness here. Yet at the same time, during the long farewell discourses (chapters 13 to 17), John has Jesus telling his followers that they are no longer slaves but friends. This is a radical shift in the way the divine human relationship is to be understood. Gods were authoritarian beings which must be obeyed, much like the relationship between masters and slaves. This is no longer to be the case. Instead, relationships of mutual trust and respect are to be the new reality (Jn 15:12–17).

Now that we have in a general way rehearsed the chronological and theological development of the four gospels it is time to focus more specifically on their resurrection material. We can then reflect on the relationship between them and Paul's understanding of resurrection. Again, we will work chronologically.

Mark only gives us one brief story. Three women go to the tomb with burial spices on the morning after the Sabbath and are wondering about moving the large stone over the entrance. When they get there the stone has already been laid aside. Upon entry the body is no longer there, rather there is a mysterious young man. They find this situation alarming. The young man tells them not to be afraid and gives them a message including the declaration that Jesus has been raised. The young man encourages them to return to Peter and the other disciples with instructions the to go to Galilee where Jesus will meet with them. The reaction of the women was, 'So they went out and fled from the tomb, for terror had seized them; and they said nothing to anyone, for they were afraid' (Mk 16:8). This experience of fear and terror does not sit well with Paul's notion of revelatory insight. It is almost the opposite of hope, joy and wonder. This fear and terror are reactions of people whose world has been suddenly undermined in ways that they do not understand, all they can do is run for a place of safety and normalcy, if such a place still exists. While after sufficient time and space for reflection the experience of the women may become re-evaluated as something more like Paul's revelatory understanding, Mark has nothing to say about this. However later writers offered alternative endings to Mark's Gospel attempting to take the story further. However, these alternative endings (as included in the NRSV) all reflect material contained in Luke-Acts and Matthew). Because we know that both Luke and Mathew as based on Mark, these ancient, amended copies must have been from a significantly later time and give little new insight.

If we turn to the other three Gospels, we find that the empty tomb discovered by women associated with Jesus, tradition is picked up and extended. Matthew inserts a prologue where a group of soldiers are sent to guard the sealed tomb to prevent any possible theft of the body which might have been seen as resurrection. This means he also has to introduce a means by which this guard could be circumvented. There is an earthquake and instead of the mysterious young man we have "an angel of the Lord, descending from heaven," whose appearance was like lightning, and his clothing white as snow. The guards are terrified, and the tomb opened. The message to the women is much the same as Mark's. However, the feelings are not, the fear is now mixed with great joy and they do exactly what they were told to do. They carry the news of resurrection and the command to meet in Galilee to the disciples. On the way to the disciples the women are briefly met by the risen Jesus who reiterates the instructions for the meeting in Galilee. Matthew also inserts a story about the bribing of the guards to tell a false story about the disciples stealing the body. Matthew then ends his gospel with the meeting in Galilee and commissioning of the disciples to make disciples of all nations. It is also worth noting that Matthew's account of the crucifixion also contains signs and wonders, an eclipse of the sun, another earthquake, the tearing of the temple curtain and the opening of graves. In the ancient world great events were supposed to be accompanied by signs and wonders. In this sense all of this type of material would have enhanced the credibility of Matthew's story. However, for many people today whose worldview follows the enlightenment and the expansion of a much more scientific view of the world the opposite effect is more likely to be the case. Scepticism rather than conviction.

Luke, like Matthew also extends Mark's brief account by having the women deliver the message to 'the eleven and all the rest.' (Lk 24: 9b) However they are met with scepticism. Peter runs off to the tomb to check for himself. After this Luke inserts the story of Cleopas and an un-named disciple who have heard the rumours but don't know what to make of them. They are on the road from the city towards Emmaus and meet a stranger who engages them in conversation about the rumours regarding Jesus. The stranger begins to explain what has happened to Jesus using the Hebrew scriptures. They invite the stranger to eat with them when they reach an inn. It is only when the stranger breaks the bread to begin the meal that they recognise him as Jesus and then he vanishes, and they rush back to join the other disciples in Jerusalem. When they get there Jesus appears again, first eating a piece of fish to prove he is not a ghost, and then does essentially the same thing as in the Emmaus story, 'Then he opened their minds to understand the scriptures' (Lk 24: 45). Luke's gospel then concludes with a commissioning and ascension. The way Luke's post resurrection accounts read it seems as though all of this happened on the same day yet, in his second volume, Acts, he says that there were forty days in which Jesus appeared and taught them about the Kingdom of God before he ascended into heaven.

John's gospel also has the tradition of the empty tomb but does not include any mysterious messenger there ready to give instructions. In fact, he only has one woman, Mary Magdalene who immediately on seeing that the tomb is empty runs off to tell Peter and the other disciple whom Jesus loved that Jesus' body has been taken. Whereupon these two, run to verify the situation. Peter, it seems did not understand the situation as resurrection, but the beloved disciple did believe. Both then went home. Mary, however, remains at the tomb, weeping. It is at this point we get the two angels who simply ask her why she is weeping, she answers them, 'they have taken away my Lord and I do not know where they have laid him'. She then turns around and another man asks her the same question, she supposes he is the gardener. Jesus then calls her by name and the moment of recognition happens. After this she is sent with a message for the disciples, but it is not about Galilee. It is about ascension and therefore about transformed relationship to the God Jesus saw as father. This changed relationship is not just about Jesus, it is also about believers like her and the disciples. Mary immediately goes and announces to the disciples, 'I have seen the Lord' (Jn 20:18). The scene then shifts to the closed room where the disciples are sheltering. There are two appearance stories at this location, a week apart. The first of these two occasions Jesus breathes upon the disciples the Holy Spirit commissioning them for ministry. Thomas is absent on this occasion. When he hears about it, he is sceptical. The second appearance is about dealing with this scepticism from Thomas. Thomas is offered the opportunity to touch Jesus' wounds. This proves unnecessary. He makes a declaration of faith.

Theologically the Thomas story deals with the theme of doubt and belief. A theme that is very contemporary and important to understanding John's Gospel. The following two verses (often understood as the original ending of John's gospel) make this clear.

> Now Jesus did many other signs in the presence of his disciples, which are not written in this book. But these are written so that you may come to believe that Jesus is the Messiah, the son of God, and that through believing you may have life in his name (Jn 20:3–31).

It is not known if the writer of John's gospel had access to any of the three synoptic gospels but given that it is generally regarded as the latest of the four, and significantly later than Mark, it is possible although there is not much textual evidence in support of this. However, this short concluding passage indicates an awareness of other ways of telling the story. It also goes some way towards an explanation of why John's gospel is so different to the other three in both its theology and style.

This brings us to chapter 21 of John's gospel. Many commentators regard this chapter as a later addition to the gospel. However, unlike the alternate endings of Mark this chapter is contained in all known manuscripts, indicating its composition as very soon after the rest of the gospel. Unlike the other resurrection stories in John this does take place in Galilee. Firstly, it references the story of a remarkable catch of fish that in Luke's gospel is associated with the calling of the first disciples (Lk 5:1–11). This story seems to function as a rehabilitation of Peter who earlier during the arrest and trial of Jesus had three times denied his association with Jesus. Three times Peter is asked by Jesus if he loves him. Three times Peter responds emphatically the Jesus knows he loves him. After each affirmation Peter is charged to feed Jesus' sheep and lambs. After this Jesus gives a short prophesy about Peter's future and calls him to 'follow me'. Peter then asks Jesus a question about the 'disciple whom Jesus loved'. He is rebuked and again commanded to follow Jesus. There is also some question about the death of the unnamed disciple who may have died sometime before the gospel was written. Yet verse 24 claims that this disciple is the writer. How could this be? Let us remember that this is an ancient document and there was no copyright law or any expectation of making money out of it! That this unnamed disciple is considered the writer may be because its content is quite possibly attributable to the teaching of this unnamed disciple who may well have been the founder of this particular early Christian community. He is not named possibly because he is one who always gave due priority to Jesus and so did not want to put himself forward as having some sort of independent authority. This scenario allows us to see him as the real author of the gospel even if it was actually written down some time after his death. It was still seen as his true testimony.

The Gospel Accounts through the eyes of Paul

Having taken a look at all the variety different ways in which the resurrection of Jesus is handled in at the conclusions of all four of the Gospels, all post Pauline, some by a considerable length of time, it is appropriate to see how they look in terms of his earlier understanding of resurrection.

For Paul the crucified Jesus has been raised up and is alive in a new imperishable way through God's breath as the principle of life. The risen Christ for Paul is not a resuscitated corpse but an imperishable spiritual body that has been transformed by God's breath. This kind of body is no longer constrained by corruption and death, by the normal limitations of mortality. In a sense it has a transcendent character going beyond normal physicality. It is a new creation.

Mark's brief account is enough to open the possibility that Jesus is alive and indicate that there has been a fundamental change to the world without attempting to define to closely what exactly has happened. He leaves us with a wide-open space into which fear of the unknown penetrates. Mark has been telling the story of Jesus' ministry and its conclusion in crucifixion. In the very first verse of the gospel Mark says, 'the beginning of the good news of Jesus Christ the Son of God' (Mk 1:1). There are only two other occasions where Mark uses the Son of God designation for Jesus. In chapter five the unclean spirits in the possessed man call Jesus, 'Son of the Most High God.' And the third is on the lips of the Centurion at the moment of Jesus' death (Mk 15:39). Throughout the gospel narrative Jesus' self-designation is the non-controversial Son of man, meaning something like the human one. In a strong sense the Gospel narrative is bracketed by the Son of God designation. Yet this same Son of God continues to be alive for Mark. He can't just end his narrative with the centurion. How is this good news if he stops at the moment of death and burial? So, he adds the briefest of narratives to affirm that Jesus is alive without further explanation. In this sense Mark is observing the same sort of restraint that Paul does on the issue of resurrection.

The other three gospels in extending their resurrection stories beyond Mark include a physicality to the risen Christ that at least enables a recognition of the crucified Jesus. However, this is a physical Jesus that does not obey normal physical rules. He appears to be able to appear and disappear when and where he pleases. This Jesus seems to, at least in this aspect, manifest something of the transcendent nature of the resurrection body that Paul puts forward in chapter 15 of the letter to the Corinthians.

I do not want to suggest that these extended stories are simply the invention of the later Gospel writers. There may well have been some widespread oral traditions that had developed by the late first century from which some stories were selected and shaped by the gospel writers in ways that helped their respective readers to gain important insights into resurrection faith. Nor would I want to dismiss the value of some insights, such a Luke's grounding of the newness of the gospel message in a fresh interpretation of the Hebrew scriptures (Emmaus Road story) or John's focus on the importance of faith and belief. (The dynamic of the Thomas story and the priority of the beloved disciple as first to believe.) Nevertheless, the stories ought not to become distractions from the revelatory nature of the risen crucified one insisted upon by Paul.

There is one further issue from Luke most notably, but also present in John. That is the idea of ascension. Luke has two versions of the ascension, one at the end of his gospel and another at the beginning of Acts. John uses the word in Jesus' conversation with Mary Magdalene in the garden beyond the empty tomb. 'I have not yet ascended to the Father' (Jn 20:17). Ascension seems to function as formal ending process to the appearances of the risen Christ. Luke set the time frame of these appearances at 40 days. In John, if we hold chapter 20 as the original ending, the time frame is only one week. This is a very short time frame to come to terms with something so extraordinary. It would also rule out any sort of resurrection encounter for Paul altogether. Perhaps this is why Luke styles Paul's experience as a conversion. All this makes me wonder if John and Luke were dealing with issues around an over emphasis on 'signs and wonders'. To me ascension appears to be about distancing the risen crucified one from creation after a brief visit. Not an idea that would appeal to Paul. How would we be able to experience life in Christ and Christ in us as Paul encourages us to if Christ has become distanced in this way?

If we look at the context in with the two accounts of resurrection that Paul gives us, we will see that he is dealing with an attempt to limit Christian freedom on the one hand and an over enthusiasm on the other. In both cases it is as though the Galatians and the Corinthians have forgotten the heart of the Gospel that he has preached.

In the case of the Galatians Paul has heard that some people have come arguing for all Christians to convert to Judaism if they wanted to sure of their salvation. To Paul doing this would amount denying the gospel of salvation by faith in the crucified risen one, as a return to being under law and so a reversal of their newfound freedom in Christ. Controversy around this issue seems to have been a significant issue during the first generation of the church. Paul tells the Galatians that he had to argue the case of salvation by faith on his second trip to Jerusalem where he met with a larger group of leaders. In the end they agreed with him. Such that he can say, 'There is neither Jew nor Greek, slave nor free, male nor female, for you are all one in Christ Jesus' (Gal 3:28). 'For you were called to freedom, brothers and sisters; only do not use your freedom as an opportunity for self-indulgence, but through love become slaves to one another' Galatians 5:13.

In the letter to the Corinthians the problem is almost the opposite. The wonder of the richness of spiritual experience and gifts has led to one-upmanship division and disorderly behaviour. Paul applies the same solution to this very different situation. He reminds the Corinthians of the centrality of love. (I Cor 13).

In Chapter twelve Paul is dealing with spiritual gifts which he understands as gifts of the Holy Spirit that are distributed amongst the congregation such that no one has them all, but everyone has something. Using the metaphor of a body made up of many parts the tells them,

> Now you are the body of Christ and individually members of it. And God has appointed in the church first apostles, second prophets, third teachers; then deeds of power, then gifts of healing, forms of assistance, forms of leadership, various kinds of tongues. Are all apostles? Are all prophets? Are all teachers? Do all work miracles? Do all possess gifts of healing? Do all speak in tongues? Do all interpret? But strive for the greater gifts. And I will show you a still more excellent way (I Cor 12:27–31)

Paul then goes on in chapter 13 to relativise all these wonderful gifts by insisting on the primacy of Love in all that is said and done. 'And now faith, hope and love abide, these three, and the greatest of these is love' (I Cor 13:13). In the following chapter Paul singles out two gifts; prophecy and tongues. Pointing out that without an interpreter for prophetic speech or a translator for tongues, nothing is gained for the listener. They cannot build up the community. The trouble with a focus on the spectacular in first instance it may simply be unhelpful, at worst it may lead to a damaging one upmanship. He goes on to encourage orderly worship. It is after all this that Pauls gives his commentary on resurrection which is not all about 'signs and wonders' but the crucified and living Christ and the love of the God he called father and the Spirit that empowers a new way of living in faith hope and Love.

When giving his list of 500 witnesses Paul says of himself, 'Last of all, as to one untimely born, he also appeared to me' (I Cor 15:8). Although Paul places himself as the last of this first generation of witnesses he is not saying that there has been a process, or event of ascension that somehow precludes the possibility of crucified and risen Christ revealing himself to others. But what he would very likely say is that such revelatory insight must take the character of the love of God as revealed in the crucified, risen one. Were this not so then how may it be said that in every generation newness of life and freedom can be experienced by those who find their lives changed by the love of God.

Earlier in this chapter we noted how the shift in timing and the change in the criteria of judgement lead to a shift in eschatological understanding beyond that of the older general resurrection of the dead on some future judgement day. That instead of a single event at the end of time we now have the breaking in of the future in the present as signs of the eschatological consummation to come. When it comes to the applicability of this new eschatological understanding the scope of Paul's understanding is cosmic in its vision such that he can say,

> For the creation waits with eager longing for the revealing of the children of God; for the creation was subjected to futility, not of its own will but by the will of the one who subjected it, in hope that the creation itself will be set free from its bondage to decay and will obtain the freedom of the glory of the children of God. We know that the whole creation has been groaning in labour pains until now; and not only the creation, but we ourselves, who have the first fruits of the Spirit, groan inwardly while we wait for adoption, the redemption of our bodies. For in hope we were saved (Rom 8:19–24a).

Chapter 12
Trinitarian Eschatology

Moltmann's Critique of Political and Theological Monotheism

Having worked our way through to an understanding of resurrection that develops into a cosmic vision of freedom that can encompass the whole of creation it is now time to explore in more depth the eschatological theme implicit in that resurrection theology. To assist our thinking, we will again turn to Moltmann. In the preface to *The Trinity and the Kingdom of God* he has this to say,

> What I should like to do now is to present a series of systematic contributions to theology differing from my earlier books in a number of ways. Here I should like to consider the context and correlations of important concepts and doctrines of Christian theology in a particular systematic sequence. I am not attempting to present a system or a dogmatics.[1]

What we get are six chapters that begin the exploration of six common theological themes through the lens of Moltmann's trinitarian theology. The last of these, chapter VI, 'The kingdom of Freedom' explores his eschatological vision. Moltmann begins this chapter with the criticism of political and clerical monotheism. His argument here Is a form of criticism of any strict form of monotheism. By strict monotheism God is seen as being a unified individual who is creator and Lord of the universe and as such having absolute authority and power over his creation. Creation is then seen as a form of property belonging to God over which he has absolute disposal. In his description of political monotheism Moltmann says the following,

---

1. Jurgen Moltmann, *The Trinity and the Kingdom of God*, (London: SCM Press, 1981). Preface, page XI.

> It is impossible to conceive of any law which is above God, for by the very nature of his being God himself embodies the highest law. If this divine sovereignty is made the prototype of the sovereignty of the state, what emerges is a hitherto unknown absoluteness of power. Theoretically, the union of the highest power and the highest law in God excludes earthly tyranny; but in actual practise the ruler's lack of accountability to anyone else puts him outside the law and 'above the constitution'.[2]

He goes on to say,

> The European absolutism of the Enlightenment. Was the final form of political monotheism in its religiously legitimated form it was also the last attempt to establish the state based on religious unity.[3]

This kind of political theology in fact it goes all the way back to the beginnings of western civilization in the first city states ruled by monarchs, Pharaohs and kings, Princes and emperors. Its clerical or religious form Is the rule of the church, or other religious structure, is the corresponding hierarchy of high priest, Pope or patriarch or priestly order. There is frequently an alliance between the two structures and in the ancient world the political ruler often doubles as a high priest.

This sort of political theology and religious theology that mirrors authoritarian structure belonging to the political realm often operates metaphysically on ideas of separation between two distinct worlds: spiritual and mundane or secular. This does not sit well with the resurrection theology that we have been exploring. It actually fits much better with the platonic separation between matter and spirit of Greek philosophy than with the holistic understanding of Jewish tradition. Even today the popular perception of theology still reflects this distortion of biblical theology, both in the churches and in the wider society. Language around death and dying is frequently framed not by talk of the resurrection but rather by this separation between body and spirit. People talk about immortal souls going to heaven or to be with God as though it was some other place quite distinct from

---

2. Moltmann. *The Trinity and the Kingdom of God*, 196.
3. Moltmann. *The Trinity and the Kingdom of God*, 196.

the creation. Whereas resurrection is not so much about us going to God as God coming to us in ever increasing fulness and finally and fully in the consummation at the end of time. As Paul says,

> For now we see in a mirror, dimly, but then we will see face to face. Now I know only in part; then I will know fully, even as I have been fully known (I Cor 13:12).

In order to resolve this issue, Moltmann makes the following statement,

> As long as the unity of the triune God is understood monadically or subjectivistically, and not in trinitarian terms, the whole cohesion of a religious legitimation of political sovereignty continues to exist. It is only when the doctrine of the Trinity vanquishes the monotheistic notion of the great universal monarch in heaven, and his divine patriarchs in the world, that the earthly rulers, dictators and tyrants cease to find any justifying religious archetypes anymore.[4]

Moltmann then asks the question, 'How must the doctrine of the Trinity be formulated if it is have this intention?'

He answers his question by outlining four points,

> (a) The Christian doctrine of the Trinity unites God, the almighty Father, with Jesus the Son, whom he delivered up and whom the Romans crucified, and with the life-giving Spirit, who creates the new heaven and the new earth. It is impossible to form the figure of the omnipotent universal monarch, who is reflected in earthly rulers, out of the unity of this Father, this Son and this Spirit.
> (b) If we see the Almighty in trinitarian terms, he is not the archetype of the mighty ones of this world. He is the Father of the Christ who was crucified and raised for us. As the Father of Jesus Christ, he is almighty because he exposes himself to the experience of suffering, pain, helplessness and death. But what he *is* is not almighty power; what he *is* is love. It is his passionate, passible love that is almighty, nothing else.
> (c) The glory of the triune God is reflected, not in the crowns of kings and the triumphs of victors, but in the face of the

---

4. Moltmann. *The Trinity and the Kingdom of God*, 197.

crucified Jesus, and in the faces of those of the oppressed whose brother he became. He is the one visible image of the invisible God. The glory of the triune God is also reflected in the community of Christ: in the fellowship of believers and of the poor.

(d) Seen in trinitarian terms, the life-giving Spirit, who confers on us the future and hope, does not proceed from any accumulation of power, or from the absolutist practise of lordship; he proceeds from the Father of Jesus Christ and from the resurrection of the Son. The resurrection through the life-quickening energy of the Holy Spirit is experienced, not at the spearheads of progress, but in the shadow of death.[5]

In the light of the Pauline theology that we have worked through previous chapter Moltmann's theology is clearly on the right track here. Its focus is firmly based in the risen crucified Jesus. What we need to do next is to see how this works out eschatologically in the story of creation.

Moltmann's Trinitarian Eschatology

Moltmann goes back to a twelfth century abbot, Joachim of Fiore, to find inspiration for a trinitarian eschatology. Joachim is one of the rare theologians in church history to develop an eschatology that has four stages perceptible from within creation. These are the Kingdom of the Father, the Kingdom of the Son, The kingdom of the Spirit and the Kingdom of Glory. These stages are not to be seen as totally distinct historical eras. Rather, they all interpenetrate each other and are kingdoms of the one God. To see them as independent would lead not to a trinitarian understanding of God but to tritheism.

Each of these divine Kingdoms is characterised by particular relationships between God and creation. The Kingdom of the Father is characterised by the relationship of master and servant. In this kingdom the Father is seen as Lord of creation and thus as having control over the whole process. Creation is brought into being for God's own purpose. The master servant relationship is hierarchical, and the power relations are unequal. However, there are servants who are coerced into obeying orders from their master, like it or not.

---

5. Moltmann. *The Trinity and the Kingdom of God,* 197-198.

There are also servants who seek to serve by their own choice having seen the something of the purposes and policies of the master. The freedom of the one who chooses service is important here. In the Hebrew Scriptures prophets, charismatic leaders and others tend to be in this second category. When we speak of Jesus as the Servant King this is what is meant (Phil 2:5–11)

The Kingdom of the Son is characterised by the relationship of parent and child. There is a relational shift here from being a servant in the household of God to becoming by adoption a member of the family of God. In the letter to the Romans Paul writes,

> When we cry Abba! Father! it is that very Spirit bearing witness with our spirit that we are children of God, and if children, then heirs, heirs of God and joint heirs with Christ—if in fact we suffer with him so that we may also be glorified with him (Romans 8:15b–17).

Here we see that the relational status becomes both higher and closer.

The Kingdom of the Spirit is characterised by a friend with friends. During the farewell dialogues between Jesus and his disciples in John's gospel Jesus says,

> I do not call you servants any longer, because the servant does not know what the master is doing; but I have called friends, because I have made known to you everything that I have heard from my Father (Jn 15:15).

This change in relationship comes after the promise of the 'paraclete' or Holy Spirit who will be the one who remains with and empowers both the disciples and those who will come to believe.

Moltmann also points out that in the history of theology that the one that is frequently missing is the Kingdom of the Spirit. It does not disappear entirely but is subsumed into the Kingdom of the Son. How does this happen?

The issue with the Kingdom of the Spirit this relationship of friendship is supported by direct mutual access to God. This sometimes allows people to claim to have received new revelations and to support this by evidence of spiritual gifts etc. If we recall the discussion of I Corinthians in the previous chapter where Paul is dealing with issues around the proper use of spiritual gifts, in particular gifts of prophesy and tongues, in the building up of the community we can see how over enthusiasm can lead in unhelpful directions. Paul was deeply emersed in the traditions of his people. There was a long tradition of prophecy in the Old Testament and alongside it a tradition of discernment between true and false prophets. Was the prophetic word consistent with what was already known by revelation (Torah) or not? Awareness of this allows Paul to focus on love as a tool of discernment as it is central to the revelation he had received.

In his earlier section on Clerical Monotheism, Moltmann tells us that in the early church, post the apostolic age, wandering free prophets were becoming a threat to the unity of both congregations and the unity between congregations. He tells us,

> It was at that time that Ignatius of Antioch formulated the principle of the episcopate which has remained valid in many churches until the present day: one Bishop—one church. He founded this episcopal unity of the church by means of the following theological hierarchy: one God—one Christ—one bishop—one church. The bishop represents Christ to his church just as Christ represents God… The doctrine of the monarchical episcopate certainly brought unity into the Christian churches, but it did so at the cost of eliminating the charismatic prophets. The Spirit was now bound to the office.[6]

This trend towards confining the Spirit to the church's leaders begins to increase over time, especially when church and empire become allied in the interests of social and political unity. While this is understandable it does not mean that Joachim's four kingdoms scenario can be seen as heretical. Trinity and the eschatological resurrection of the dead are included in the historical creeds and therefore are a part of the core doctrinal teaching of the church. However, there is an increasing divergence between official teaching and the day-to-day practical governance of the church as an institution allied with secular governance. So long as Joachim's theology does not result in some sort of popular radical movement it can simply be ignored and the practical subsummation of the Kingdom of the Spirit into the Kingdom of the Son can continue. Moltmann's trinitarian approach to eschatology means that this subsummation of the Kingdom

---

6. Moltmann. *The Trinity and the Kingdom of God*, 200.

of the Spirit can no longer be simply ignored but must be seen as empowerment by God in the present age.

In his discussion of the dimensions of Freedom that are made real in the Kingdoms of the Father, Son and Spirit Moltmann makes the following comment in relation to the Kingdom of the Spirit.

> Up to now we have interpreted freedom either in the relationship between subject and object, as lordship, or in the relationship between subject and subject as community, fellowship. But there is a third dimension too: freedom in the relationship of subjects to a *project*. Without this dimension freedom still cannot be comprehended. In relationship to the project of the future, freedom is a creative initiative. Anyone who transcends the present in the direction of the future in what he thinks, says and does is free. Seen theologically, this is the special dimension given by the experience of the Spirit. In the Spirit we transcend the present in the direction of God's future, for the Spirit is the 'earnest' or 'pledge of glory'.[7]

The Kingdom of Glory is characterised by a relationship of full immediacy and full knowledge as described by Paul, 'so that God may be all in all'. (I Corinthians 13:12, 15:28) When I reflect on this kingdom of Glory, I find it difficult to go beyond these simple phrases from Paul. I do not know the 'how' and the 'when' of this transformative Kingdom when the hole creation becomes the home of the triune God and of all creation. The very inclusiveness of this vision just gives me a sense of hope sustaining me even through times of despair. In a sense it keeps me living and that is enough.

Creation as God's Project

In the previously quoted passage above, Moltmann is describing creation as God's project which is not yet fully realised or completed. It is still ongoing and in which all creatures, including human beings, are participants, each in their own way. When creation is seen as a project then we need to see the process, from initial conception to its final goal.

When I first retired from full-time work it coincided with a decision by one of my sons to move with his family to Launceston, some two

---

7. Moltmann. *The Trinity and the Kingdom of God*, 216–217.

hours' drive away. This meant that family get togethers would require overnight stays by somebody. The five of them came down to visit for a couple of days during the Christmas New year period. We discovered that our house which had been largely designed for a retired couple as a three bedroomed house was somewhat overcrowded with seven people in it, especially considering the children were still quite young!

There were two options. We could look at some sort of extension on the existing house or put up another smaller building further up behind the existing ones. Having been involved in doing an extension to an existing building before I knew it could be both more complex and much more disruptive than building a totally different structure. It would be very likely that an extension could also be more expensive and have unexpected budget issues. To be able to afford to do this in retirement I would need to be an owner builder. So, I did the owner builder course and also got my white card so as the allowed on a construction site. I also decided to buy a kit for an ancillary dwelling or 'granny flat'. It included all the plans, a screw together frame, and all the exterior cladding for the outside walls. It was a bit like the kits for stand-alone garages or large sheds. An old mate of mine, my younger son and I had all had some experience of doing sheds and a history of helping each other out on various projects. I had the beginnings of a team which would also help keep the labour cost down. I would also have to organise all the specialist trades and pay for those with real money. So, the whole project looked workable without having to borrow more from the bank.

The whole project took about eighteen months. We reached what is called the lock up stage about halfway through the project. This is the point at which the building has become weathertight. The foundations, the structural frame, the external cladding and roofing, windows, and eternal doors; all of these things have been done. About half the budget has also been expended. There is still a great deal to do before the project can be seen as a finished dwelling in which people can make a home. It is at this stage that one can wander about inside and begin to sense what life could be like to live in the various spaces and rooms. There are hints of the life to come when it can be dwelt in.

When we use this building project image it is possible to think of creation as God's building project where God is building Godself a home. In the present we are at something like the lockup stage. We can get a sense of where things are going but the project is not yet complete, the time when God can move in is still a way off.

The question that arises here is, what is God's motivation to engage in this creation project? For Moltmann this question is answered through God's self-designation as love. 'The theology of the divine passion is founded on the biblical tenet, 'God is love' (I John 4:16).'[8] Moltmann then goes on to propose some theses to explore this theme of 'God is Love'. We will not quote the full four-page section but only enough to get a sense of what the self-designation as love means for God and creation.

> *Love is the self-communication of the good.* It is the power of good to go out of itself to enter into other being to participate in other being and to give itself for other being . . . Love wants to leave and to give life it wants to open up the freedom to live that is why love is the self-communication of the good without self-renunciation and the self-giving of the good without self-dissolution.[9]

> *Every self-communication presupposes the capacity for the self-differentiation.* The lover communicates himself. He is the one who communicates and the one communicated. In love he is both simultaneously . . . if God is love he is at once the lover, the beloved and the love itself.[10]

> By *deciding* to communicate himself, God; his own being otherwise his decision would not be self-communication of the good which he is. If he *discloses* his inner being through his *decision*, then his being, his goodness and his own being flow into this decision, and through that into the world. God communicates himself to other being not out of compulsion and not out of some arbitrary resolve, but out of the inner pleasure of his internal love:[11]

> God is love means in *trinitarian* terms: in eternity and out of the very necessity of his being the Father loves the only begotten Son . . . the Son responds to the Father's love through his obedience and his surrender to the Father. The Father and Son are alike divine beings, but they are not identical . . . The

---

8. Moltmann. *The Trinity and the Kingdom of God*, 57.
9. Moltmann. *The Trinity and the Kingdom of God*, 57.
10. Moltmann. *The Trinity and the Kingdom of God*, 57.
11. Moltmann. *The Trinity and the Kingdom of God*, 58.

> inner trinitarian love is therefore the *love of like for like*, not the love for one who is essentially different . . . like is not enough for like. If it's free and creative love is responded to by those whom it calls to life, then it finds its echo, its answer, its image and so it's bliss in freedom and in the Other. God is love. That means he is engendering *and* creative love. He communicates himself to his like *and* to his Other. God is love. That means he is responsive love both in essence *and* freely . . . That is why we have indeed to see the history of creation as *the tragedy of the divine love*, but must view the history of redemption as *the feast of the divine joy*.[12]

> Creative love is ultimately suffering love because it is only through suffering that it acts creatively and redemptively for the freedom of the beloved. Freedom can only be made possible by suffering love. The suffering of God with the world, the suffering of God from the world, and the suffering of God for the world are the highest forms of his creative love, which desires free fellowship with the world and free response in the world.[13]

The final theses needs to be quoted in full.

> This means that the creation of the world and human beings for freedom and fellowship is always bound up in the process of God's deliverance from the sufferings of his love. His love, which liberates, delivers and redeems through suffering, wants to reach its fulfilment in the love that is bliss. But love only finds bliss when it finds its beloved, liberates them, and has them eternally at his side. For that reason and in this sense the deliverance or redemption of the world is bound up with the self-deliverance of God from his sufferings. In this sense, not only does God suffer with and for the world; liberated men and women suffer with God and for him. The theology of God's passion leads to the idea of God's self-subjection to suffering. It therefore also has to arrive at the idea of God's eschatological self-deliverance. Between these two movements lies the history of the profound fellowship between God

---

12. Moltmann. *The Trinity and the Kingdom of God*, 58–59.
13. Moltmann. *The Trinity and the Kingdom of God*, 60.

and man in suffering—in compassionate suffering with one another, and in passionate love for one another.[14]

For Moltmann, love is the motivation for project creation. To be more precise the self-designation of God as love requires the creation of the other, the stranger, in order that the fullness of love can be realised. In this sense it is necessary that this other has the capacity, the freedom, to speak both the yay and nay to its creator. This will involve both suffering and unfairness in which both Creator and creature learn suffering love, the love of the cross which resolves the burden of pain suffered by creation and creator and so liberates both. All of this requires time and space in which to grow and become and eventually realised in the fullness of the Kingdom of Glory.

Before we conclude this chapter on Moltmann's eschatology it is important to note that there are aspects of his theology that remain controversial. We could launch into a deeper exploration of some of these areas of Moltmann's theology, but it is enough for our purposes to understand that his four kingdoms approach does allow us a way to see a real possibility that at the end of the day our issue with the wraerggowrapper designation will find ultimate resolution. In that sense there is hope.

---

14. Moltmann. *The Trinity and the Kingdom of God*, 60.

Part 4 Reflections on the Journey

Chapter 13
Bringing the Threads Together

Reflecting on Christian Theology in an aboriginal way

It is now time to reflect, in an aboriginal way, on the Christian theology that has been expressed throughout the third section. But first let us recall where Woorrady's theology left us at the end of the second section. We will try to see how the three theological thoughts expressed at the end of the second section can be expanded in ways that further illuminate the themes expressed in them. It will be helpful to think about these three thoughts in a different order to the way we arrived at them.

We can affirm that the typology of struggle between the stability and sustainability of Moihernee and the capacity to go badly wrong represented by Wraerggowrapper is still valid as a way of understanding a wide range of issues in the present day. This is particularly relevant to climate change, loss of biodiversity, plastic pollution, acidification of the oceans and depleted availability of fresh water. I would also include here those human behaviours and systems that are major contributors to this situation.

This thought represented by Wraerggowrapper was reflected on from a variety of different perspectives. We looked at the 'problem of evil' and 'protest atheism' in western philosophy. Then we asked about ways in which science might also help us to illuminate this persistence of the Wraerggowrapper designation. In the process we came to understand that elimination of this Wraerggowrapper designation, within the process of creation, could not be entirely achieved. This was particularly clear when we looked at the science around freedom and necessity within creation. We then turned to biblical and theological discussion of these issues. From these discussions we did learn that we should not get involved in trying to blame the victim for their misfortune. We also learned from Moltmann's trinitarian theology of the cross, that God understands the pain and suffering, which creatures sometimes must endure. There is empathy in the heart of God for the suffering we experience. However, there is always an encouragement to do what we can to mitigate and diminish suffering by working to counter the Wraerggowrapper designation. We can do this through risk management as a way to minimise the opportunities for things to go wrong. We can also avoid any blaming of the victims of misfortune. Instead, being open to offer them compassion, empathy and love. We can also raise a cry against injustice whenever it is clear that human action is a major causative factor in the suffering of others.

In this way we have be consistent with the aboriginal approach to knowledge. An approach that seeks to see the connections between different forms of knowledge and so gain a sense of the whole. In this process deeper wisdom is gained. Everything is connected.

In his 1838 sermon Woorrady points us towards the Christian doctrine of creation and salvation without any sign of having become a Christian. He uses the word God, which he knows will mean the Christian God both to his aboriginal audience and the British colonisers, when he speaks of creation. He ends this sermon by saying, 'Love him and you go to him'. I suspect that here we see him interpreting what he knows about Christian beliefs on the afterlife as something similar to his traditional beliefs where the spirits of the dead return to country/land after death.

This return to country/land after death is sometimes thought about as reincarnation. However, it is better thought of as a kind of recycling. The wholeness of a person's life is in this sense never lost, but returned to country where it can be made available in the lives of future generations.[1] Paul's theology of the resurrection also enabled us to see something similar. His insistence on resurrection as revelatory and as being holistic in terms of the resurrection body (soma pneumaticon) leads to the understanding that the wholeness of creaturely life is to be caught up in the eschatological consummation at the end of time and so included in the home of God. So, the idea that nothing is ever truly lost sits in the background of both Woorrady's and Paul's Theology. These eschatological ideas also indicate the final

---

1. Langton & Corn, *Law*, 140-1.

removal of the Wraeggowraper designation. The final transformation of completed creation becoming the home of the triune God also resolves all issues of justice and unfairness so characteristic of the present world we know.

We noted the capacity of Woorrady's creation stories to change as the situation with country/land changes. This capacity indicates that we need to see Woorrady's theology as an open system. A theological system that is open to and relevant to the world of today, which is very different to the world he experienced some two centuries ago.

I would also say that the theology of both Paul and Moltmann that we have discussed above are open systems. The three theologies are both relational and adaptable to changing circumstances. Woorrady is able to adapt his stories to track major change observed in country and to also point towards a possible future for his people. Paul is able to take his revelatory experience of the risen crucified Jesus and see how this anticipates the eschatological future in ways that give a greater fullness to living in the here and now driven by faith, hope and love. Moltmann's trinitarian theology is also very relational and adaptable as expressed through his eschatological vision of the four kingdoms.

The theology presented here and the theologies of Woorrady, Paul and Moltmann are whole of Creation theologies. Once we take seriously the idea of creation as the activity of a God who chooses to designate Godself as love and so engages in a project of creation, as building Godself a home in which to dwell, this includes creation as the other who is loved, and so fulfills God's chosen designation as love, then it is no longer possible to believe that such a God could in any sense fail in this purpose. This is an unashamedly universalist statement. In examining Paul's theology based on the revelation received that the crucified Jesus had been raised from the dead by God, not only changed the timing of resurrection but also the criteria of judgement away from a crime and punishment model to a restorative one based on grace and love as expressed in Christ Jesus the crucified one. God has acted in an all or nothing way in the cross of Jesus taking up into Godself all the pain and suffering of creation. Because of this salvation is also to be seen as an all or nothing exercise. Nothing is ultimately lost. All has a place in the home of God, in the Kingdom of Glory. We are drawn into the project of the triune God.

These whole of creation theologies have some consequences for our spirituality. They imply a universal understanding of salvation. We are not just talking about human beings here (or a subset of people who have the 'right' faith or understanding), but the whole creation. If the tiniest microbe is not included, then neither am I. This is both humbling and liberating. I am loved and valued in the same way that the Triune God loves and values the whole creation. It would not be the same without any part of it. All is valued and loved by this Creator God as a part of the glorious home he builds for Godself and for creation. This is humbling because it provides my true value which is both marvellous and somewhat less than my ego sometime imagines. This is liberating because I no longer need to be concerned about whether or not I am good enough to be worthy of love. Instead, more energy can be focused on relationships outside of myself with the rest of creation. I can do this on the basis of recognising the truth in the assumption of my ancestors that everything is related.

Instead of adopting the Kingdom typology from Moltmann's eschatology, I would suggest that instead of referring to the 'Kingdom of God' we consider speaking of the 'Ecology of God'. Moltmann's four-part eschatology would then be the 'Ecology of the Father', the 'Ecology of the Son', the 'Ecology of the Spirit' and the 'Ecology of Glory'.

As we saw earlier Moltmann's four-fold eschatology is about the complex inter-relationships of the Triune God and Creation, and the way in which those relationships unfold as project Creation proceeds. Understanding it ecologically creates a space and a meaningful intergenerational purpose for all of us that is equitable and not dominated by the pursuit of power and wealth. It values Aboriginal history and insight as powerful teaching from which all can learn love of country. It also focuses our attention on the whole complex interrelationships of planet earth as the home of all its living creatures. It is about justice and fairness for all creatures. A genuine ecological theology draws no harsh distinction between human society and its ecological home such that exploitation is made to seem ok, even necessary. Ecological theology is also about the whole of creation explicitly. It pushes us in the direction of being humbler about our own expectations as we seek to create safer more sustainable communities.

Curiously, working through this project I have developed a theology that gives some underpinning for a t-shirt slogan observed at the most recent Uniting Aboriginal and Islander Christian Congress national conference. It read, '100% Aboriginal, 100% Christian'. I can hold to both traditions because as whole of creation theologies they can be seen as being essentially the same thing; just approached from different viewpoints. This thought and practice could possibly be extended to other systems of belief and practice if they also take a whole of creation approach and remember the mantra that everything is connected.

We can now return to the context in which this theology and spirituality has been constructed. The context is the complex challenges of climate change and the other externalities that have been brought on by the ways our mainstream human civilisation has developed. There is now a growing urgency to find other ways of doing human civilisation that are much more sustainable.

Reflections on the Ecological challenges to our current way of life

In the first part of this book, we began to get a sense of the gravity and size of the challenge that climate change, and all the other externalities, presents for human civilisation on earth. We also gained an understanding of some of the deep drivers within our current style of civilisation that have contributed to the current situation and are still driving it to become worse before it can get better. We concluded that the changes to the ways we do civilisation needed require us to reshape human civilisation in transformative ways such that it is given a new identity. There is a need to reimagine the future. One thing seems to be self-evident. The future however we approach it is going to be far less conducive to human civilisation than the past ten thousand years has been. Planet Earth is going to be less predictable in its climate and less resilient in its capacity to cope with its human members. Our environment is becoming more hostile so, whatever else happens, we will have to pay it much closer attention.

So, let's get our imagination going in what might be termed a thought experiment. We will do this by imagining two basic scenarios. One that looks into the future where the basic drivers of our current global civilisation continue to operate in a 'business as usual' way even as we try to transition away from fossil fuels and rely on technology to save the day. The second scenario will assume a change from 'business as usual' towards aboriginal ways of thinking where everything is connected, country is a first teacher, and economics changes its goal from endless growth to building a 'safe place for humanity'. We will call this second scenario 'a more hopeful path'.

Let's start with the 'business as usual' scenario. The most recent meeting of the G20, representing the world's largest national economies, were all still seeing economic growth as measured by Gross National Product as the goal. The myth of continuous growth in a finite world still prevails even though the mounting pressure of adverse climate events, such as droughts, floods, heat waves and wildfires, is effectively showing us that the overall fruitfulness of planet earth provides for its' human population is at risk. These adverse events are also bad for agricultural production. A flood, or large storm, can destroy a whole productive season. Heatwaves and drought can also seriously affect agricultural production. If these events are to become both more frequent and extreme, then the risk of widespread famine will also increase pressure on humanity and its current form of civilization.

The 'business as usual' scenario is also fuelled by the pursuit of material wealth via the intergenerational accumulation of such wealth. This is a dynamic which fuels economic inequity, which in turn leads social inequality and a sense of political disenfranchisement. These are issues that can lead to serious destabilisation of politics and society. We here in Australia are not immune from this. A recent issuing of a quarterly statement of the national accounts showed a small increase in GDP largely fuelled by high levels immigration. When these numbers were described on a GDP per capita basis the result was a decrease. This means that many of us got a little bit poorer, an increase for social and economic inequality. This inequality is also a global phenomenon.

The final report to the United Nations by its climate change scientific advisory group indicated that close to forty percent of the earth's human population is already at risk of adverse climate events. If we further assume that this risk will grow before it can get better, then where are these billions of people going to go? It is highly likely that we will see a huge increase in migration, both legal and illegal. At the moment most of the migrants who are on the move are motivated by the perception that a better life is to be had in Europe, North America and, to a lesser extent Australia and New Zealand. This is largely because these destinations have had higher standards of living and long periods of stable governance. However, the climate does not recognise national borders. There have already been heat waves, wildfires and catastrophic floods impacting these destinations. These destinations also have high levels of social and economic inequity, and in turn lower levels of confidence in institutions and governance leading to higher levels of instability. The safe place for humanity represented by Kate Raworth's doughnut is looking much more like a tiny chain of islands in a vast ocean rather than a broad space of safety for humanity.

Within this scenario there is a lot of potential for conflict. Rising inequity and the sense of disenfranchisement increases the risk of internal conflict within nation states. Similar forces also increase the potential for dangerous conflicts between nation states. The more we continue down a path that fosters competition over cooperation increases the risk of open conflict and destabilisation around the globe. There is a high risk of a catastrophic collapse of civilisation from which recovery will be both difficult, costly and will probably take much longer.

Let's now turn to the second scenario, to 'a more hopeful path'. In this scenario the future of civilisation considers both reimagining political theory and economic policy. It also takes a lead from ancient aboriginal thinking. In particular the idea that everything is connected, the understanding of country as our first teacher, and that good leadership is about building a consensus for the good of the whole community.

Perhaps the first step in this 'more hopeful path' scenario is to recognise that the 'business as usual' model of mainstream civilisation has already reached its use by date and simply cannot continue without potentially dire consequences. If we can't see the problem, we can't even begin to try and fix it!

The next step is to take the aboriginal advice to see the environment as our first teacher. In other words, to pay a lot of attention to the environment in which we live, and especially to the environmental science community. All too often mainstream civilisation has not done this sufficiently well enough. Instead of really focusing on our environment as first teacher our civilisation has developed in such a way that we are more inclined to reshape the environment to suit our needs and desires. This is instead of trying to understand it such that we might adapt to it. This can lead to insights about how we might gradually reshape our world in ways that enhance environmental resilience at the same time as increasing its productivity for humanity.

There is a connection here with the problem of growing inequity. I once heard a frank admission by a conservative political commentator that went something like this, 'the natural supporters of conservative politics are those who have something they don't want to lose'. This something can take various forms which at the end of the day amount to some sort of perceived advantage in the current ways society operates. This advantage might be economic, political, or social privilege. As such there is a strong resistance to any reform or policy that seeks to change the current ways of doing things even if strong evidence is presented that such change is both needful and urgent.

Making fundamental change to the way human civilisation works may seem an impossible task. Working to create such immense change appears as a daunting challenge. So, lets break it down a bit and see how it is possible to work towards appropriate change. The challenge is obviously a global one. But it also has local impacts and requires a change of attitude, or perspective at a personal level. This is why I often ask myself about what I am currently doing in relation to these three different levels. In doing so I try to remember the ancient principle that everything is connected. The big picture and the small space of my own activity are related to each other.

Taking the big picture first, what am I doing that is connected to this? The first and most obvious connection is the writing of this book. Through this book I'm attempting to make connection to people anywhere in the world who might find inspiration to continue their journey towards a different more sustainable future for humanity and ecosystem Earth, or perhaps begin some first steps in that direction.

Second, almost a decade ago now we began planning to build an energy efficient house for our retirement. As finances allowed, we have since installed two solar energy systems and now export about four times as much green energy into the grid than we draw out. Now someone somewhere else connected to the east Australian grid is benefiting from the availability of that surplus green energy.

Third, The, propagation and planting of a couple of hundred trees and shrubs on our property over the past eight years or so has begun to draw down carbon from the atmosphere. The amount may seem small against the scale of the huge amount of carbon dioxide still being pumped in from the use of fossil fuels, but it is still a contribution in the right direction. The growing of a significant amount of our own fruit and vegetables also lessens dependence on the supermarket and its supply chain where dependence on fossil fuels is still a significant item.

When it comes to the local community level, I am less connected than I used to be before retirement. Despite this I can still be supportive of others whom I know share similar concerns about the harm being done to the planet and they ways in which it unfairly affects the poor and vulnerable people in our community. And I am also thankful for the support that is given to me by other local community members. Because Australia is a democracy, I also have the privilege of being able to vote from time to time in Federal, State, and local government elections. This means I can learn about the candidates and their policies and so decide on which candidates are most likely to advocate for reforms that have a greater likelihood of leading humanity towards a more sustainable future.

At a personal level there are two things that I would like to mention which are potentially able to be taken up by others. The first is what I call 'learning to love the country you are on' and the other the theology and spirituality that enables us to face the daunting future with courage and hope.

Over a decade ago we were living in Launceston and all our children had become independent and retirement was less than a decade away. Consequently, the topic and manner of retirement became a more significant feature of our conversation. Eventually, it was decided that the location for our retirement ought to be in the southern Midlands on the outskirts of the broader Hobart metropolitan area. This was because we had spent four years in Oatlands and a further eleven years in Moonah, part of the northern suburbs of Hobart. This would allow us to reconnect with people we had known during those years and with family members who lived reasonably close by. So, we set a budget and started looking for a block of land we could afford. Most of the blocks we looked at were either too expensive or too isolated. Eventually we found one that was just a little over our budget and about the right size and in a mutually agreeable location.

As it turned out we ended up building on the property and living there much sooner than we had anticipated. Not long after we had signed the contracts for the block, I was involved in a traumatic incident which set off an emotional breakdown and I was diagnosed at severe risk of major depression and was off work on medical grounds for over five months while receiving psychological counselling. In the end it was decided that it would be unsafe to return to work in the same placement and I was transferred to the Bridgewater/Gagebrook parish mission, not ten minutes' drive from the block. Just over a year later we moved into our new house.

I had already known quite a bit about the story of this lower Jordan valley, reaching all the way back into its 40,000-year pre-colonial human history, such that I can still look out onto the landscape in a way that sees through the current day-built infrastructure and see the ancient aboriginal roadways between the hills along which clans moved from season to season between their estates. However, it was only in beginning to live here that I began to understand what it means to see country as first teacher and to love the country I live on.

This is not easy country on which to plant trees and shrubs to enhance and build the complexity of the ecosystem. The soils are shallow and compacted from years of sheep and cattle grazing. Average rainfall is around 300 millimetres per year. Country soon taught me that you can't simply dig a hole, plant something and expect it to thrive. There may be a need to improve the conditions. This could include thinking about raising and improving the quality the soil. Questions arise about efficient use of water and the frost and drought tolerance of the plants you may want to use. In the first couple of years, we were here many of the plants we tried did not do well at all. Country was teaching me what worked and what did not. All the while, as I learnt, my relationship with country grew such that some habits of a lifetime began to change. All the solo bushwalking and fishing in the high country that I used to think of as being on country began to lose its attractions. I was becoming much more connected to the place where I lived. I was learning to love the country I was on, even though it was much smaller and largely lacking in the sheer power and grandeur of the mountains. Here wonder and joy, was to be found in the collecting of seed and the propagation of plants and in the small creatures that were coming back to live here. Learning to love the country we are on turns out to be a very significant and meaningful thing to do. I recommend it as an important strategy in reshaping our mindsets for a more sustainable future.

Having got this far hopefully readers cannot fail to have noticed that the Christian theology presented in this book is significantly different from that which is presented in most Christian communities, and in the popular notions about Christian belief in the broader society. It is not the older 'carrot and stick' variety of the colonial missions that Woorrady encountered, nor is it a 'ticket to heaven' where heaven is seen as some place entirely other than the creation in which we happen to live. Where heaven is an otherworldly place, we go to after death provided, we have the 'right belief'. Some might criticise this form of whole of creation theology as being too universal, passive and failing to provide sufficient motivation to do good and seek justice. This is not so. If we understand creation as God's project to give expression to his love and to build Godself a home among all his creatures, then we would want this future home to be the best possible home for all of us. So, we would want it to be just and equitable for all its inhabitants, for all creatures great and small.

Currently I am part of what must be the Uniting Church in Australia's smallest Parish Mission and one of its smallest congregations. We have also passed through fire and flood quite literally on the way to our present form. These days we are imbedded in the building from which the Uniting Church welfare operates its services in one of most disadvantaged suburbs of Hobart. We worship each week in the facility's multi-purpose room. The gathering is a small one. There are twelve to fifteen regular participants. Many of us have experienced poverty and personal trauma of one kind or another. We seem to be quite good at empathy and mutual support. The theology of the group is non-judgemental and open to a broad range of perspectives. I have been involved with this unique small Christian community on and off for two decades now. Despite all obstacles it has developed into a community of extraordinary healing power for those who have been traumatised and emotionally broken, including me. These days I'm not the Minister. I seem to be more of an elder in both the Christian and aboriginal sense, and a de facto grandpa for the youngsters. In some ways this community, small as it is, is becoming a model for the kind of society we need to become if we want to face the future with simple courage and hope.

As we move forward into this long period of change and uncertainty as outlined in the first section there is a need to continually remind ourselves that everything we say and do will have some sort of impact through the networks of relationships which we inhabit, even small things. Rather than behaving in ways that seek to accumulate material wealth and power as individuals and families we should seek to build our relational wealth. Firstly, by simply recognising the relational reality of our lives. Secondly by enhancing and strengthening those positive relationships we encounter. This is about changing the goal of our lives towards a more sustainable future.

Voice

I am writing this section in the immediate aftermath of Australia's constitutional referendum seeking to enshrine both recognition of and a voice for its first peoples. The referendum failed in all states on a roughly forty to sixty percentage basis. Right from the start the question put to the Australian people did not have bipartisan support. The major conservative parties opposed the referendum proposal to recognise first peoples in the constitution by way of giving them an advisory voice to government on matters that concerned their longstanding disadvantage. The request for such a voice arose out of a long consultative process led by aboriginal people that culminated in the 'Uluru Statement from the Heart'. This statement was not directed to government but directly to the people of Australia. Constitutional recognition and voice, however, is not the full agenda of the statement but merely one important suggestion for a means of dealing with a much larger agenda of issues that Australia needs to work through if we wish to have a more just and inclusive society. I, like the bulk of my aboriginal brothers and sisters, was disappointed by the result, but have become even more committed to the Uluru agenda. This agenda includes truth telling, treaty, lament and hope for our children, disadvantage in health, education, meaningful employment, and a commitment to unceded sovereignty. Remembering that an aboriginal understanding of sovereignty is radically different from the mainstream understanding of national sovereignty.

Across all of these items there are aboriginal voices which will continue to advocate for change in one way or another. The Uluru agenda is real and will not go away without substantial progress. Many small community-run aboriginal organisations will no doubt pick up or continue to advocate on parts of this larger agenda. It would have been good to have a national voice to pick up some of this work from these small community-based organisation so that they could focus more energy on the good work they do in their communities. At this point I do not intend to pick up the entirety of the list. There are two items that I do wish to comment on. They are notion of sovereignty used in the Uluru Statement and the hope for our children. We will start with sovereignty. The Uluru Statement describes aboriginal sovereignty in this way.

> This sovereignty *is a spiritual notion: the ancestral tie between land or 'mother nature', and the Aboriginal and Torres Strait Islander peoples who were born therefrom, remain attached thereto, and must one day return thither to be united with our ancestors. This link is basis of the ownership of the soil, or better, of sovereignty.* It has never been ceded or extinguished, and coexists with the sovereignty of the Crown.[2]

This is both a theological statement and a statement about deep relationship. This is much more so than it is a claim to a piece of international law on sovereignty. It is impossible to hear or read this expression of sovereignty without thinking about the nature of the relationship between Aboriginal people and Country. In the preceding paragraph (to the one quoted above) the statement about the spiritual nature of aboriginal sovereignty is given a context. This context is given in terms of deep time. This deep time is described in a multifaceted way. It is described as 'from the Creation', in the reckoning of Aboriginal culture, from 'time immemorial' in common law and 'more than 60,000 years' according to science.

It is this depth of relationship between people and country that is foundational to Aboriginal identity. This relationship to country is the basis of how Aboriginal civilization worked, persisted and eventually thrived, throughout a long history of environmental and climate challenges. Even the flora and fauna was radically different to

---

2. *The Uluru Statement from the Heart*, made by aboriginal and islander representatives from all parts of Australia in 2017. This italicised quote was brought into Australian case law, by the High Court, as a part of the judgements in the land rights cases, Marbo and Wik, in the 1990's.

anywhere else on earth. For Aboriginal people, learning to live with country was fundamentally important. The relationship with country was and is the most significant thing for life and community. As always country is the first teacher. All aboriginal faith and spirituality, all hopes for the future, the very sense of who we are as Aboriginal people, of our identity as a people, are bound to this relationship with country. So, when I think about this spiritual notion of sovereignty, which has never been ceded, I can't see how it could disappear while there's one aboriginal person and there is one piece of country. Thinking about sovereignty in this sense is not the same as it is in international law sense. You can cede sovereignty in international law sense, when you surrender after invasion or something like that. But ceding sovereignty understood in this spiritual sense would amount to a denial of ourselves as a people with a long and deep history on this continent.

I would suggest that this 'sovereignty' is not founded in the crowning of kings, or the conquest of the lands of others, or in constitutional conventions or referenda, or any other human political construct. Rather it arises out of country in all of its ecological reality and includes its human members as a part of that ecological system. This is quite unlike the usual meaning of the word with respect to nation states. This aboriginal notion of sovereignty raises a serious challenge to the idea of the absoluteness of the power of nation states to determine what happens inside their borders. In the changed world we are entering into we can no longer afford any notion of a right to absolute control of what happens within national borders. Ecosystem earth does not respect such borders. What happens in place has impacts on the whole system. This has to change. The nations of the world can respect this fact and learn to co-operate much more effectively. Not to do so commits us to catastrophic collapse of any form of human civilisation.

I want to turn now to hope for our children.

> When we have power over our destiny our children will flourish. They will walk in two worlds and their culture will be a gift to their country.[3]

---

3. Uluru Statement from the Heart, 2017.

Here we see a concern by leaders and elders for future generations in an increasingly uncertain world. There is also talk about living in two worlds. To me this is often experienced as an uncomfortable tension. I do not look like an aboriginal person in any obvious way. There is enough European ancestry in my family tree to appear white. This means that I do not experience any obvious racism when I simply walk down the street. However, when people find out about my connection to aboriginal Tasmania the reactions can vary quite a lot. For some it is just some sort of interesting fact, but for many the reaction is one of mistrust as though I have betrayed them in some way, and 'let the side down'. This kind of racism can be very corrosive of one's basic sense of personal identity and capacity to trust other people. If this is what living in two worlds is about then it would be something that I would not want to pass on to my grandchildren. However, this interpretation of 'living in two worlds' does not need to be the only one. Instead, we can see it differently.

If we understand this two worlds passage in an aboriginal way, then we are seeing two worlds, or civilisations, co-existing in the same space. It then becomes a question of the relationship between the two and how that might be improved. What shall we keep and what needs to go? At the moment there seems to be a tacit assumption, by many, that the path for everybody should be go with the majority. Or at least stick with the 'business as usual' way of doing things. The trouble with this is that a significant minority may become disenfranchised, and some very good ideas may be taken off the table to the detriment of the whole. In this sense the relationship is not working. There is little real deep listening going on and the opportunity for substantive change is never really on the table. Consultation is just a process step before there is a change that we didn't ask for. The Voice was meant to be a way to prevent this all-too-common style of consultation process.

Instead of this one-sided approach there needs to be mutual listening in order to discern better ways forward. There needs to be a searching for negotiated outcomes by parties who are mutually respectful of each other's wisdom.

Megan Davis, an aboriginal constitutional law professor, who was part of the leadership group for the Uluru process, writing her Quarterly Essay, 'Voice of Reason', has this to say,

> Uncle Stan Grant Snr once said of language, it's not who you are, but where we are. Uluru is not about identity politics. It's about location. We are located on this land together. We coexist. The Voice to Parliament is not just about the parliament and the executive. The parliament and the executive are representatives of the *people*. It is a Voice to the People. It is a dialogue for time immemorial between First Nations and the Australian people.
>
> We live in an era of rapid incontrovertible climate change. Our old people want peace for their country. This is a moment of transformation. It is a time for renewal. People are sick of the tired, feral, aggressive arguments of the past. They want progress on integrity, climate and indigenous lives.
>
> The Uluru statement is an invitation, a gift to the Australian people. When people say this is about changing Australian identity, it is not. It's about location; we are located here together, we are born here, we arrive here, we die here and we must coexist in a peaceful way. We're about to face a serious existential crisis as a people, as humankind, as the climate changes and the planet warms up. The fundamental message that many elders planted in the Uluru Statement is that to face this battle together, the country needs peace, and the country cannot be at peace until we meet; Uluru Statement is the beginning of that.[4]

Oddly enough the word, 'peace' does not appear in the Uluru Statement, yet it is at the heart of the quoted passage written by Megan. She wrote this essay as a part of the campaign for the referendum. Despite the defeat of the referendum the truth of her statement here is still relevant. We must meet in good faith and mutual respect for the sake of our children and for the planet which gives us life.

---

4. Megan Davis, 'Voice of Reason', in *Quarterly Essay*, 90(2023): 64.

Bibliography

Paul Davies, *The Cosmic Blueprint* (Sydney: Allen & Unwin, 1989).

Megan Davis, 'Voice of Reason', in *Quarterly Essay*, 90(2023).

Elizabeth Finkel, *The Genome Generation* (Carlton: Melbourne University Press, 2012).

Bill Gamage, *The Biggest Estate on Earth* (Crows Nest: Allen and Unwin, 2011).

Hans Kung, *Does God Exist?* (Oxford: University Press, 1978).

Marcia Langton & Aaron Corn, *Law* (Port Melbourne: Thames & Hudson, 2023).

Nicholas Clements, *The Black War* (St Lucia: University of Queensland Press, 2014).

John Hick, 'The problem of Evil', in *Philosophy and Contemporary Issues*, edited by John R Burr and Milton Goldinger, Second Edition (New York: Macmillan, 1976).

Jurgen Moltmann, *Experiences of God* (Philadelphia: Fortress Press, 1980).

Jurgen Moltmann, *The Crucified God* (London: SCM Press Ltd, 1974).

Jürgen Moltmann, *The Trinity and the Kingdom of God*, (London: SCM Press, 1981).

Bruce Pascoe and Bill Gamage, *Country*, (Port Melbourne: Thames & Hudson, 2023).

Bruce Pascoe, *Dark Emu*, (Broome: Magabula Books, 2014).

NJB Plomley, *Friendly Mission second edition* (Hobart:Quintus Publishing, 2008) and *Weep in Silence*, (Hobart: Blubber Head Press, 1987).

Alistair Rae, *Quantum Physics: Illusion or Reality* (Cambridge: Cambridge University Press, 1986).

Kate Raworth, *Doughnut Economics* (London: Penguin, 2017).

Henry Reynolds, *Fate of a Free People* (Camberwell: Penguin Books, 2004).

HH Rowley, *The New Century Bible Commentary—The Book of Job* (Grand Rapids: Eerdmans, 1980).

Lyndall Ryan, *Tasmanian Aborigines a history since 1803* (Crows Nest: Allen & Unwin, 2012).

Bernard Brandon Scott, *The Trouble with Resurrection* (Salem: Polebridge Press, 2010).

Pavan Sukhdev, *Corporation 2020* (London: Island Press, 2012).

Brian Walker, *Finding Resilience,* (Clayton South: CSIRO Publishing, 2019).

Tyson Yunkaporta, *Sand Talk* (Melbourne: Text Publishing, 2019).

www.ingramcontent.com/pod-product-compliance
Ingram Content Group UK Ltd.
Pitfield, Milton Keynes, MK11 3LW, UK
UKHW010326280625
460175UK00004B/20